SELECTED POEMS OF
LUIS CERNUDA

Edited and Translated by
REGINALD GIBBONS

UNIVERSITY OF CALIFORNIA PRESS
BERKELEY   LOS ANGELES   LONDON

University of California Press
Berkeley and Los Angeles, California

University of California Press, Ltd.
London, England

ISBN: 0-520-02984-4
Library of Congress Catalog Card Number: 75-3767

Two of these translations first appeared in *Stonecloud*
and one in *Ironwood*.

Printed in the United States of America

Translator's dedication:

For my parents, and in
memory of my grandmother,
Sophie Lubowski

CONTENTS

■ *Contents*   ix

PREFACE

I wish to express my gratitude to the Comisión Fulbright of Madrid and the Fulbright Commission of the United States, for awarding me a grant in 1971-1972, when I began work on these translations; to Dan Lube, for his liberal aid to me that year; and especially to Donald Davie, for his generous, careful — and, for me, indispensable — scrutiny of the manuscript version of this book.

I also wish to thank Jean Franco and Gareth Reeves for many helpful suggestions concerning the introduction and the translations, respectively.

Neither mistakes of translation nor of judgment, however, should be attributed to any of my benefactors, but to me alone.

R. G.

Princeton, N.J., 1977

INTRODUCTION

I

Luis Cernuda came of age in a country that was continuously in the throes of crisis and governmental failure, from Spain's loss of the war with the United States in 1898, through its military dictatorship of the 1920s, and the proclamation of the Republic in 1931, to the terrible civil war of 1936-1939. Later, as an exile, Cernuda watched from a distance the long and harsh period of economic recovery which never in his lifetime returned political freedom to a people who have enjoyed very little of it in their history. In the first decades of this century, intellectuals did oppose both political constriction and the conformism of Spanish society. Intellectual life, however, was characterized not only by an intense scrutiny of Spain's melancholy social history, a new interest in the ideas and attitudes of the rest of Europe, and a feverish though marginal avant-garde literature, but also by an almost total isolation from the centers of authority and power within the nation.

Cernuda, born in Seville in 1902, certainly registered the sense of exclusion and ineffectualness, and the strains of an age of anxiety, as acutely as his fellow poets in what is known in Spain as the Generation of 1927 (Lorca's *Poet in New York* was written in 1929, Rafael Alberti's *Concerning Angels* the year before, Cernuda's own surrealist volumes in 1929 and 1931). Literary life then meant mostly life in Madrid. Cernuda went there in his mid-twenties, found the availability of elegant clothes and literary conversation to his liking,

1

and avidly enjoyed jazz and the movies. But he also suffered from a lack of money and from that epoch's deadening intervals of ennui, which Cernuda alone among his contemporaries articulated. Rapidly, between 1927, the year of his first book, *Perfil del aire,* and 1936, when *La realidad y el deseo,* his first collected volume, appeared, he tried a number of poetic styles and strategies. Like many other writers, he allied himself in the meantime to the Republic and for a while answered in a small way its unusual invitation to intellectuals to help reform and govern the country. But Cernuda's hatred of Spanish bourgeois society was not lessened by the change of government. Although in 1934 he joined, for a brief time, the Communist party, it was his rebelliousness that made him a temporary Communist, not his political consciousness that made him rebel. When later he wrote of enduring the bombardment of Madrid's University City by Franco's forces, it was to recall that at that moment he had discovered Leopardi, whom he read as the shells were bursting nearby. Cernuda's temperament was resolutely antiauthoritarian, anti-institutional, and by the time he left Spain he had become in essence politically inactive. What is most impressive, however, is that it is in his war-year poems, *The Clouds* (1937-1940), that he finds his mature style and is able to write of the war itself, to transcend the more intimate lyrics of his earlier work, and to gather men and history in his net. But it was distance, perhaps, which helped him. Early in 1938, through a friend in England, he obtained a temporary teaching position in that country. When he returned as far as France in July, he found the way to Spain closed, as the ill-financed, ill-governed Republic declined before the inexorable modern warfare of the Fascists. Cernuda went back to England to begin the exile that would last for the rest of his life.

Highly principled, unsociable, dandified, very much an autodidact, homosexual, both grateful and grudging toward his literary elders, certain of his poetic powers — Cernuda became quite early in his own mind a *poète maudit.* And he would not, however painful it may have been for him, renounce his personal history as the substance of his poetry, for he believed that the integrity of a poet's life and work depended on his faithfulness to what he recognized himself to be and to what he was still on the road to becoming. Perhaps Cernuda's love of Goethe came out of his similar sense of the fulfillment of the individual. As Fredric Jameson succinctly summarizes it, Goethe's "vision of the full development of the personality . . . neither aims to break the personality upon some purely external standard of discipline, as is the case with Christianity, nor to abandon it to the meaningless accidents of empirical psychology, as is the case with most modern ethics, but rather sees the individual psychological experience as something that includes within itself seeds of its own development, something in which ethical growth is inherent as a kind of interiorized Providence."[1] Cernuda found himself, in fact, halfway between the static repressive codes of the bourgeois Catholic society within which traditional literary life was conducted, and the pure reactions to chance or to history which were the respective paths of the avant-garde aesthetic and the social revolution of his time.

The authenticity for which Cernuda strove, itself imposed rigorous demands on him, without regard to the impression he made on others. So he went his own way always, bringing his rebelliousness, his eroticism, and his quest for self-knowledge to his work as the very touchstones of self-acknowledgment. Thus the movement of his poetry is from the early creation of a self-contained mood of melancholy and subversive narcissism, to meditation on a full world of men and things, gods and history, all of them manifestations of troubled times, past and present.

II

Within the history of Spanish poetry, Cernuda represents some marked departures (not all of which he effected alone): he adopted a colloquialism in his poems which was not intended to suggest a "low" and therefore humorous or ironic style, but rather a high seriousness; he thoroughly explored the relationship of "spiritual purity" to "poetic purity," as he put it; he introduced the modern dramatic monologue into Spanish poetry, though his monologue is rather different from that of his professed model, Browning. His themes included — along with his obsession with solitude — a serious treatment of both narcissism, which may have appeared earlier in Spanish literature, and homosexuality, which had not. His youthful rebelliousness against Spanish society led him to seek out Gide and the French surrealists as models for his writing. In both his poetry and his criticism he brought Spanish poetry into touch with the English Romantics, as well as with more recent English and American poets; and his criticism was neither belles lettres nor impressionism nor mere erudition — all of which might have been expected of a man of letters of his time in Spain — but rather had a clearly stated aesthetic and moral basis, which included a sense of the relationship between the spoken and the written language, and wide and intelligent reading of European poetry.

What must be added, however, is that these facets of his work — which are, in fact, some of its virtues — must inevitably seem most significant when seen entirely from inside the literary history of the Spanish language. That Cernuda's work was both different and new can be seen in the range of responses it elicited; on the one hand Juan Ramón Jiménez commented with characteristic irritation and hauteur that Cernuda's poetry seems to be a translation from English, while on the other hand both critics and poets commend Cernuda for his conscious sense of himself as a European, not just a Spanish, poet.[2] But if by about 1925 the writing of poetry in English had reached a point that required a renunciation of Romantic attitudes, Cernuda was able to bring those attitudes to fruition in a country and in a tradition that had not produced any very important Romantic poet, with the possible exception of

Bécquer.³ Not merely the music and sense, then, but also the historical impact of Cernuda's poetry requires some rehearsing in English.

"Concealed under the Romantic manner," wrote Boris Pasternak, "was the conception of life *as the life of the poet.* It had come to us from the Symbolists and had been adopted by them from the Romantics, principally the Germans" (my italics). This narrowing of the idea of life, which at the same time makes a grander claim for poetry itself, is the most durable trace of Romanticism in our century — the difference being that the value placed on life itself has declined, perhaps, in the face of historical atrocity, technological dehumanization, and the difficult status of the arts, which are always prey to commercialism and ideology. Pasternak believed that, although figures like Yesenin and Mayakovsky had found this Romantic conception of life amenable, it was no longer possible for him. But his description of the Romantic manner offers a striking summary of Cernuda's position, and perhaps it is more than mere coincidence that it does:

> In this poet [Pasternak writes, of Blok] who sets himself up as the measure of life and pays for this with his life, the Romantic conception is disarmingly vivid and indisputable in its symbols, that is in everything that figuratively touches upon Orphism and Christianity . . . . But outside the legend [of the poet], the Romantic schema is false. The poet, who is its foundation, is inconceivable without the non-poets to bring him into relief, because this poet is not a living personality absorbed in moral cognition, but a visual-biographical "emblem," demanding a background to make his contours visible. In contradistinction to the Passion Plays which needed a Heaven if they were to be heard, this drama needs the evil of mediocrity in order to be seen, as Romanticism always needs philistinism and with the disappearance of the petty bourgeoisie loses half its content.⁴

In quoting Pasternak, who is hostile to the Romantic manner, I do not mean to imply that Cernuda's position is false. Indeed, we will see that the difference between

the Russian and Spanish traditions in this respect is that
Cernuda's Romanticism legitimately opposed itself to a
philistinism of indisputable power (nor, one should add,
is it likely that philistinism disappeared in Russia with
the "disappearance of the petty bourgeoisie") and was
in fact fully engaged in a moral struggle with the world
around it. But Pasternak touches on a number of points
that also appear in Cernuda's work, not least among
them the analogy to Christian drama, for it is worth
noting that Cernuda's utter rejection of Christianity and
orthodox morality, though militantly insisted upon in
many poems, was in some sense impossible for him to
achieve fully. The role of the *poète maudit* – the singer
unheard in the wilderness or the prophet unheeded in
his own land – is a role whose very provenance is
Christian, whose significance depends on its implied
analogy to the roles in the Testaments of preacher and
Messiah. Cernuda *was* in earnest when he rejected the
church, when he rejected God, but in order to reject
them, he had to use them. And in the late poems the
rejection has, sadly, come to be merely a gesture, as the
uncertainties of age and loneliness finally prove, per-
haps, too terrible.

To return to the Cernuda of the vigorous early and
middle work, however, is to encounter an analogue of
Baudelaire. The adoption of an evil that depends for its
definition on the existence of the good, and which
indeed consecrates that good by opposing it, is an ines-
capable paradox for both poets. Baudelaire's alexan-
drine elegance articulates attitudes that are inimical to
the tradition from which the alexandrine itself comes,
inimical to the social world which still views the alexan-
drine as a proper poetic vehicle. And Cernuda's rejection
of conventional "good" must seek its own ideal in
Greek antiquity or in physical beauty, which themselves
participate in the established aesthetic order.

There can be no mistaking the allusion in the first line
of Cernuda's "The Poet's Glory" to Baudelaire's "Au
Lecteur." Both poets recognize themselves precisely in
what they hate, both reject the established morality in

order to discover anew that moral truth that freedom at once confirms and subverts. The assertiveness of solitude, which Sartre points out in Baudelaire, is present in Cernuda, too.[5] And for Cernuda part of the attraction of Gide and the French surrealists was their sense of some higher ethical norm than the conventional, and their assertion of their painful freedom as the practice logically required by this ethical theory.

"Romanticism always needs philistinism," writes Pasternak. One can imagine Cernuda replying, "As if there were ever any shortage!" This theme, which is vitally important to Cernuda's work, is again the representation of a dialectical tension: if the Romantic is opposed to the philistine, then in some way he admits the necessity of the philistine as the foil to his work. But one must go beyond Pasternak's phrase to the practical evil wrought by the philistine. For all Spaniards on the side of humanity, Lorca's death was the shocking reminder of the power of that evil:

> Just as one never sees bright petals
> Spring from rock,
> Thus among a hard and sullen people
> There is no proud new ornament of life
> To flower in splendor.
> For this they killed you . . .

With these lines Cernuda opens his poem on Lorca's murder. There are other times when, beyond what one might ordinarily identify as philistine, "reality" itself seems philistine, even in its natural manifestations, when these do not seem to proffer respect to beauty or to the transcending moment that breaks the bars of time. The disdain one sees in this attitude is tempered, however, after Cernuda's exile, which first gave him cause, I believe, to conceive of an audience whose attention was vital to him. Not that he wrote exclusively *for* a distant Spanish audience, but that he turned to address them and in so doing confronted new poetic problems that, as *The Clouds* and *As One Awaiting Dawn* show, were fruitful indeed. Cernuda found a voice that was public without being declamatory; his poetry became more accessible without losing its stylistic energy.

What of the German Romantics, whom Pasternak also mentions? Is there a connection here too with something in Cernuda's work? If one considers the social context of Cernuda's Romanticism, then the truth is that the political parameters of his rebellion and that of the German Romantics are somewhat akin. Consider the similarities between the marginal position of Germany in nineteenth-century Europe and Spain's similar position in the twentieth century. In addition, note that the artistic disenchantment that characterized Spain's new literature in this century is unlike the disenchantment one finds in the more advanced, industrialized countries — England, the United States, or even France. Spain is to some extent the receptor of literary innovations from abroad which, transplanted to Spain, cannot be the same as they were in their country of origin. To take one important point, there is literally no substantial petty bourgeoisie in Spain in the 1920s whom a writer might shock — instead he aims to shock a greatly reduced number of fellow writers (who are difficult to impress) and members of high society. The political and social freedoms which have been won already for the bourgeoisie in other nations are here hard-won by the artists themselves. And, in the ensuing confusion and ambivalence, one sees a writer like Cernuda turning, like some German Romantics, not to present-day social causes or Utopian conceptions for his inspiration but instead to idealized realms of the past, like ancient Greece.[6] Perhaps it will not surprise the reader to find that in the 1930s Cernuda felt a great affinity with Hölderlin, and even translated some of his poems into Spanish. Cernuda's admiration for the German is not narrowly literary, but instead grounded in a profound sympathy for Hölderlin's personal and social struggles. As Cernuda writes, "on various occasions, in his youth, Hölderlin made several attempts to submit to the rules of conventional society: the sufferings of his servitude, half professional, half domestic, among well-to-do families, must have been terrible."[7]

In the early essay from which this quotation is taken, Cernuda's distaste for the mass of men (again, the philistine), is no more apparent than his worship of the ideal figures of youthful beauty who suffer at their hands: "The epoch in which Hölderlin lived presents us with a heroic world, shaken by profound historical emotions, occasionally transfixed by radiant young lives snuffed out before reaching their midday, as in the fate of mythological youths." Cernuda also writes wistfully of "a life that is lost in the modern world, and for whom the secret forces of the earth are the only realities, far from the conventions by which society is governed — rules that were prolonged and ennobled by other poets, but which someone like Hölderlin could never acknowledge without negating himself and vanishing."[8] Thus one sees many figurative and explicit statements in Cernuda's poetry of the antithesis of philistine versus orphic or prophetic poet.

To conclude these correlations with Pasternak's analysis of the Romantic manner, we must draw a distinction between his description and Cernuda, for Cernuda — perhaps unlike the poets Pasternak had in mind — was very definitely "absorbed in moral cognition," as many of his writings show, and as he himself reiterates. So absorbed was he as to place "poetic thought" at the center of his verse, and to subordinate imagery and diction to it in every case. There was, however, in his steering clear of the intense subjectivity of Juan Ramón Jiménez, also an avoidance of the opposite pole: that "objectivity" which, in the Pound of the Pisan Cantos, for example, has been called "the capacity for sympathetic identification with inhuman forms of life, . . . an attitude of reverent vigilance before the natural world."[9] Cernuda's preoccupation with human ethics made it impossible for him to regard natural phenomena as independent of the human observer. For him they must always be actions and entities whose significance is symbolic, casting an exemplary light back on human affairs. As one critic remarks of Cernuda's mature verse, "the objects of the world should never determine the poem, but should be subservient to the philosophical imagination, and not the fancy."[10] The ethical concern is central because the human is central, rather than the natural world of which, other poets might hold, man is only a part.

If the human is central, then it is the fate of man which colors all reflection. Thus the elegiac tone that comes to dominate Cernuda's middle and late works. Octavio Paz would even maintain that all of *Reality and Desire* is an elegy:

> In neutral tones of pearl grey, the poet begins by singing the force of desire, which aspires to fuse itself with reality, but like the wave which falls back from the shore, carried by its own fateful movement, he ends by singing, not the desperation of desire but its nostalgia, the nostalgia of the wave for the beach. Thus the lyric, without ceasing to be personal, loses that egoism, that individualism, of more recent poetry. Cernuda's book is something more than the expression of his individual experiences: it seems to me that it is the elegy of a generation and of an historical moment, which are bade farewell for the last time, forever — an elegy for Spain and for a world which cannot come back.[11]

It is in this way that Cernuda, though a *poeta comprometido* (*poète engagé*) in the strict sense for only a year or so,[12] always stood against aestheticist verse, which was predominant in Spain during the 1920s and into the 1930s, and from which not even Cernuda, in his earliest work, escaped wholly. But he did not need, as did others, to "humanize" his later work, for it was never "dehumanized."

Thus, although a curious sense of distance, of diffidence, may be discerned in Cernuda's first three volumes (up through 1929), his poems nonetheless are centered on the emotions. One critic states that "out of despair, weariness, or pique, Cernuda sheltered behind expressions that leave much unsaid."[13] This refers to the poems of *A River, A Love* (1929), in which emotion is, in fact, heavily armored by Cernuda's new tech-

Introduction ∎

niques. Yet there can be no doubt that the emotions in question are vital, and that obliquity serves not to mask anything, but on the contrary to allow expression of what might otherwise remain unexpressed — one thinks of Cernuda's homosexual eroticism, for example, as well as his highly charged criticism of social mores. From the beginning, he sought to objectify or distance his material, which was simply his own life, but like Eliot, he retreated — not from sentiment — from sentimentality. While at this time Jorge Guillén or García Lorca wanted nothing in their poems which was human in the sense of being autobiographical ("anecdotal," they said), Cernuda wrote of nothing but himself, and the difficulty of the early poems is consciously presented as a defense against having to appear too nakedly in them.

It was the central importance of the human which led Cernuda to praise the work of Antonio Machado when most of his contemporaries still felt obliged to reject it as old-fashioned. For Machado had insisted on the predominance in poetry of intuition over "algebraical" reason, and had condemned the metaphorical ingenuity of younger poets as essentially rational rather than emotional, and thus not fully human.[14] For Cernuda, the modern substitute for the religious consolation of the past was precisely the human moment, the instant that brought full consciousness of the fragility of life and *therefore* of its enduring significance. There may be a sort of unconvincing Platonism behind this, but it is more likely a true tension, for these moments are both deeply felt and, unfortunately, rare, as is the moment of fulfilled human love, which is Cernuda's other great theme. If belief in the perfect moment, in beauty, often collapses, there are also many instances of being disabused of the illusion of human love. The many oppositions and tensions that we have mentioned in Cernuda's work are the emblems of *Reality and Desire:* the desire for perfection and transcendance, versus the reality of dull quotidian existence devoid of immanence; the desire for love and erotic fulfillment, versus the reality of betrayal, indifference, callousness, and the mere passage of time that wears away at affection.

Cernuda alternates between two responses to this dilemma. On the one hand, he constructs "vital lies" in which to believe for the sake of believing. On the other, he seeks out solitude and even narcissistic consolation for their own sake, as the only retreats from what is more painful. The "vital lie," such as a tension-racked half-belief in God or the gods, can be sustained for a time, but it must inevitably and regularly fall. One can mark the zenith of belief in a poem like "Violets," and the nadir in "The Poet's Glory." It is between affirmation and negation, however, that Cernuda's best poems lie, as they present both the impossibility of the ideal and the necessity for it, as in "Ruins" and "*Apologia pro vita sua.*"

III

All the events in Cernuda's life, and his temperament as well, contributed to producing his attitude of combined nostalgia and asperity. In 1950 he wrote of his friend the painter Gregorio Prieto in a passage that could stand as epigraph to Cernuda's own life and work:

When Prieto, while still young, obtained the Rome Prize, his long sojourn in Greece and Italy must have revealed to him an ideal which, little by little, would become an obsession — which on occasion would even smother his natural instinct for the real. The works he showed in Madrid in 1936 were the fruits of those years. That ideal, more than a longing for classical paganism, is a longing for a certain impossible Golden Age, symbolized on his canvases from time to time by the beautiful young bodies, naked and amorous, who populate the white ruins of the Mediterranean coast. But this attraction, which like a powerful magnet the South exercised over his imagination, has been countered by the vagaries of the times, which carried Prieto to Northern Europe, where he has lived for some years, and where the light and atmosphere must have modified not only his vision of the ideal, but his perception of the reality of things as well.[15]

It is the poet's "perception of the reality of things" rather than his sense of the "objective" existence things may possess independent of the observer which most preoccupies Cernuda, as we have noted. And as well as his sense of things as symbols *for* man, this too leads him to place man's voice at the center of his work. Most of his poems are to be read, indeed, as the utterance of a specific voice — Cernuda's own. He employs the "lyrical I" rarely (after certain early poems), which is to say that he does not often dissociate his own, human voice, from the voice of the poem. On one occasion he admitted this as a confusion that might legitimately be held against him, but, as Octavio Paz notes, even these most personal poems cannot be accused of being egocentric. And Cernuda did employ certain devices in order to create some sense of distance, particularly the frequent address to a second person, a "you" (Spanish *tú*), who is in fact himself. The effect of this is to make the poem seem a self-conscious interior monologue, a sophisticated talking-to-one's-self. The root of this strategy is Cernuda's lifelong desire to understand the relationship between the man who lived and suffered, and the maker of poems, a distinction he was led to, it seems, by Eliot.[16]

Thus, whereas Browning might speak through the mouth of a created character in order to live imaginatively what he would not present as his own experience poeticized, Cernuda's characters have Cernuda's voice: in the present selection, most notably Lazarus. Cernuda did not so much seek to delve into exotic or unusual experience in these monologues, as to impute to other figures, whether historical or created, a voice that is recognizably his own.

For again, it is personal history that lies behind all his poems: "I have always tried to compose my poems beginning with an initial source of experience, and I early taught myself that practice, without which the poem would neither seem inevitable nor acquire precise outlines or exact expression."[17] A visit to some place or person, a dead friend recalled, a landscape observed — these are the kernels of the poetic experience as Cernuda presents it. The problem of poetry is not invention, but to sort out the relationship between the spectator's experience and his continuing existence. Poems in such a vein will not put up metaphorical veils, nor resort to subterfuge in order to live out imagined or recreated feeling lyrically — at least not in Cernuda's mature work, after his avant-garde enthusiasm had played out. He signaled what is most important to him when he titled his study of the English Romantic poets *Poetic Thought in the English Lyric of the Nineteenth Century,* and his own poetry gradually moved away from purely sensuous or semantic effects toward discursive meditation.

He praised the public involvement of Yeats and condemned, in later life, the egocentric isolation of Jiménez, precisely because he felt it important for the poet, whatever his beliefs, to grapple with ideas and society. He greatly admired the *Four Quartets,* and Eliot's criticism as well, especially that which strove to establish a vital relationship between poetry and significant religious thought, though this may seem surprising given the great distance between Eliot's orthodoxy and Cernuda's unflagging antagonism to established institutions and dogma.[18] Thus one sees that for Cernuda experience must determine the poet's themes, and themes determine his choice of imagery. Therefore experience — both spiritual and social — must be his prime concern. While his early work is quite inventive, Cernuda's mature poetry is not visionary but retrospective.

His images and figures, from *The Clouds* on, are not themselves the essence of his poetry, as they might have been in earlier works, but rather adornments, something like the musical ornamentation without which even Mozart's melodies might seem too plain. He casts about until he has found what is required by the poem at a given point in order to articulate thought or feeling. The reader will perceive the trajectory of Cernuda's work as moving from the sort of Spanish poetry that Robert Bly praises for its "leaping" (*A River, A Love; Forbidden Pleasures*) to meditative poetry that is more discursive than imagistic (*The Clouds; As One Awaiting Dawn*). Cernuda's great stylistic freedom comes, in fact, not only from earlier apprenticeship to formal verse but from the early liberation of the poems of 1929-1931. Then as if swinging on a pendulum back toward an expressive center, he moved toward a style that, while retaining the free verse and flexibility of early poems, would cohere around the flux of *conscious* thought and emotion. The flaw of the last volumes (which are not given much representation in the translations) is that the pendulum's momentum seems to have carried it beyond the fruitful center to a point where the thought in the verse dominates all else, and results in a merely, and wholly, discursive poetry with little or no evidence of the keen ear and graceful articulation that mark the greatest poems.

Cernuda is perhaps Spain's best example of the *deraciné* intellectual. His earliest successes and failures as a poet were bound in time to the disintegration of his family, his definitive departure from Seville, the unease with which he tried to enter literary life in Madrid, and his sudden opportunity in 1928 to teach in France for a year. The course of his exile leads, from 1938 to the end of his life in 1963, through many cities, but it has also been said of him that he was born an exile, and remained an inner exile wherever he went.[19] Like some Spanish emigrés, he did not readily adapt to British or North American culture; unlike others, he seems to have made little effort to do so. Until the last years of his life, when in Mexico he was pleased to live among old friends from Spain, he did not have the advantage of congenial surroundings. One might guess that Cernuda's closed temperament and at times unsociable nature prohibited him from forming intellectual or emotional attachments to any place after leaving Seville. Even his affection for Seville came too late, long after he was out of Spain for good, when he recalled a childhood that was probably, in truth, not unusually happy. Again, the reality and the desire are at odds. His political convictions were individualistic and did not, after the 1930s, induce him to join any cause; nor might they have made him a very desirable recruit. His financial means were never very great, and more than once he lost them, or as in the case of a position he held at Mt. Holyoke College, voluntarily gave them up in favor of a life in accordance with his principles.

He reminds one of other inner exiles, a clan of many poets — Pasternak, Pound, Mandelstam, Rilke — whose native land was that of European culture: books. Books that in difficult times had to take the place of life itself: "For many years I was living *vicariously,*" Cernuda wrote, "and at times I would read in order to substitute something for the life I was not living." [20] At more propitious moments, life *could* be lived, and the living of it, to Cernuda's way of thinking, must always be tied to a sense of passionate intensity and complete honesty.

It is not surprising that his poetics led him eventually to concentrate his efforts on meditative poems. This was a mode of writing that could deal adequately with the details of daily existence, the movement of history and society, and his fundamentally religious longing for an instant or an object capable of transcending the confines of linear time, and mortality, but which would center its attention not on events or objects but on the human life that strives to establish itself in relation to them.

He was both exile and outcast, but the ability to write poetry "despite" one's circumstances might have seemed incomprehensible to him. For Cernuda, poetry *was* one's circumstance, and he would respect himself — and other poets — only so long as the writing of it remained a need irreconcilable with a devotion to anything else.

NOTES TO THE INTRODUCTION

1. Fredric Jameson, *Marxism and Form* (Princeton, 1971), pp. 65-66. This summary of Goethe's ethics comes in Jameson's discussion of Walter Benjamin. It is worth adding that the notion of an "interiorized Providence" comes very near to Cernuda's use of the word *demon* in "The Poet's Glory." That is, the choice in Spanish of *demonio* over *diablo* carries an etymological suggestion of great importance to Cernuda: the Greek *daimon*. This word came to mean both personality — that is, a fated relation-

ship with the exigencies of one's own character — and a god or governing spirit with whom one also stands in a fated relationship. Cernuda speaks of this in detail in "Palabras antes de una lectura" (1935), in *Poesía y literatura* (Barcelona, 1971), pp.151-156. And he concludes his autobiographical essay, "Historial de un libro" (in *Poesía y literatura,* pp. 177-216), with the Spanish translation of the words of Heraclitus: "ethos anthrōpō daimon," "Carácter es destino." It could be argued that Cernuda's understanding of these words is inapplicable to their pre-Socratic origin, but such argument would not lessen their importance in this context.

2. Jiménez is quoted by Agustín Delgado, "Cernuda y los estudios literarios," *Cuadernos Hispanoamericanos,* no. 220 (April 1968), p. 96. See Carlos Otero, "Poeta de Europa," *Papeles de Son Armadans,* Book 8, vol. 29, no. 85 (April 1963), pp. 36-49, for a reasoned argument in favor of Cernuda's Europeanness.

3. It is not my purpose to debate the characteristics and relative merits of Spanish Romanticism here, though the specialist may object; if he should, I can only point to the most obvious aspect of Spanish Romanticism, which is its adherence to what one might call the Scott/Byron line as opposed to the Wordsworth/Coleridge line, an adherence that Cernuda's case opposes. E. Allison Peers's lengthy study of Spanish Romanticism may be usefully supplemented by the middle chapters of Gordon Brotherston's *Manuel Machado: A Revaluation* (Cambridge, 1968), which neatly summarize the conflict between Romanticism and later movements in Spain. In any case, Cernuda's Romanticism was superseded, in Spanish, by Pablo Neruda's, whose powerful rhetoric, vatic authority, and proclaimed roots in the *pueblo,* as well as the absence in his work of a strong sense of the crisis of language that one finds in poets as diverse as Mallarmé, Eliot, and César Vallejo, make him the last Romantic poet, and not the least.

4. Quoted in the introduction to *Pasternak,* ed. Donald Davie and Angela Livingstone (Nashville/London: Aurora Publishers, 1970), pp. 20-21.

5. Jean-Paul Sartre, *Baudelaire* (New York: New Directions, 1967), p. 18. There is a striking resemblance between Baudelaire's prose poem "L'étranger" in *Le Spleen de Paris,* the first poem in that volume, and Cernuda's first poem in *The Clouds,* "Noche de Luna" (this similarity is caught by Carlos Otero in "La tercera salida de *La realidad y el deseo," Papeles de Son Armadans,* Book 5 vol. 17 no. 51 [June 1960], p. 438). Other correspondences crop up: Cernuda's "Noche del hombre y su demonio" (again, the *daimon*) has much in common with Baudelaire's "La fin de la journée" and his prose poem "A une heure du matin."

6. Here I briefly paraphrase Ernst Fischer (*The Necessity of Art.* [London: Penguin, 1964], pp. 56-58) on the politics of the

German Romantics; the points in Fischer's book are sometimes crudely and contradictorily argued but his work is useful.

7. Cernuda, "Nota introductoria a unos poemas de Hölderlin" (1935), in *Critica, ensayos y evocaciones* (Barcelona, 1970), p. 118.

8. Ibid., pp. 117-118.

9. Donald Davie, *Ezra Pound: Poet as Sculptor* (New York, 1968), p. 177.

10. Alexander Coleman, *Other Voices: A Study of the Late Poetry of Luis Cernuda* (Chapel Hill: University of North Carolina Press, 1969), p. 25.

11. Quoted by Carlos Otero in "La tercera salida de *La realidad y el deseo*" (see n. 5, above).

12. See J. Lechner, *El compromiso en la poesía española del siglo XX. Parte primera: de la Generación de 1898 a 1939* (Leiden, 1968), I, 94-95, 122. Cernuda actively incorporated political conviction or creed in his work at infrequent intervals; most explicitly, this appears in a previously uncollected piece, "Los que se incorporan," reprinted in *Critica, ensayos y evocaciones*, pp. 89-91.

13. C B. Morris, *A Generation of Spanish Poets 1920-1936* (Cambridge, 1969), p. 194.

14. Machado's statement can be found in the famous and very useful anthology edited by Gerardo Diego, *Poesía española contemporánea* (1932, 1934; complete edition Madrid: Taurus, 1970), p. 149. See my translation of this statement, and of other writings of Machado on poetry, in "Antonio Machado on Poetry and Literature," *The Denver Quarterly* 12, 1 (Spring 1977), 79-96. See also José Luis Cano, *Poesía española del siglo XX: De Unamuno a Blas de Otero* (Madrid, 1960), pp. 76-77

15. Quoted in Otero, "La tercera salida," p. 437n.

16. See Cernuda's opening words in the "Historial de un libro" for his conception of the "lyric I" and the "autobiographical I" (p. 177).

17. "Historial de un libro," pp. 208-209. Cernuda restated this on several occasions, and insisted that his position was tied to the ethical dimension of poetry. In St. John of the Cross, for example, "the literary beauty and purity are the result of the beauty and purity of his spirit; that is to say, the result of an ethical attitude and a moral discipline. Perhaps it is difficult to appreciate this today [1941], when there is still going around that very poor argument in favor of the purity of the rhetorical elements of the poem, as if the poetic work were not the result of a spiritual experience, outwardly aesthetical, but inwardly ethical" (*Poesía y literatura*, p. 45). Here Cernuda is distinguishing the sort of purity he means from the sort found in "pure" poetry, which, with its apparently inhuman machinery and properties, was at the center of the Spanish avant-garde from the twenties until the civil war, and which, after the war, when political poetry

18   *Notes to the Introduction* ∎

of any sort was forbidden if it did not praise the regime, was the rationalization adopted by many good poets who had to find a way of writing about their lives without any degree of explicitness with regard to society.

Cernuda's late criticism of Jiménez centered on the "narrowness of the position that Jiménez adopted, defending beauty as the only province of poetry. But, besides aestheticism, there is another, decisive field for the poetic function, which Jiménez did not take into account — always preferring as he did his own life, and putting it above all else — the field of the ethical" (*Poesía y literatura*, p. 392).

18. See "Goethe y Mr. Eliot," *Poesía y literatura*, pp. 321-330. Cernuda thought so highly of Eliot that his sojourn in England made writing problematic and publishing sheer anguish. Apparently, Cernuda sent his poems in translation to Eliot hopeful that they would please that austere editor enough for Faber and Faber to bring out an edition. They were rejected. For a brief account of this, see Alberto Adell, "El panteísmo esencial de Luis Cernuda," *Insula*, no. 310 (September 1972), p. 6.

19. Julia Uceda, "La patria más profunda," *Insula*, no. 207 (1964), p. 8.

20. Cernuda, "Historial de un libro," p. 211.

THE POEMS AND
TRANSLATIONS

VIII

Vidrio de agua en mano del hastío.
Ya retornan las nubes en bandadas
Por el cielo, con luces embozadas
Huyendo al asfaltado en desvarío.

Y la fuga hacia dentro. Ciñe el frío,
Lento reptil, sus furias congeladas;
La soledad, tras las puertas cerradas,
Abre la luz sobre el papel vacío.

Las palabras que velan el secreto
Placer, y el labio virgen no lo sabe;
El sueño, embelesado e indolente,

Entre sus propias nieblas va sujeto,
Negándose a morir. Y sólo cabe
La belleza fugaz bajo la frente.

VIII

Crystal of water in tedium's tired hand.
The clouds come back in coveys through the sky,
Over the pavement they disperse in flight
With lights half-hidden, widely scattering.

And the flight inward. The cold — reptilian
And sluggish — clenches tight its frozen rage;
Solitude, behind closed doors, begins
To throw its light across the empty page.

The watchful words that veil the enigmatic
Pleasure; and virgin lips are unaware.
The indolent dream, enraptured now,

Becomes a prisoner of its own thick mists,
Refusing to die. And nothing more
Than fleeting loveliness beneath the brow.

X

El amor mueve al mundo,
Que descansa perdido
A la mirada. Y esta
Ternura sin servicio.

Ya las luces emprenden
El cotidiano éxodo
Por las calles, dejando
Su espacio solo y quieto.

Y el ángel aparece;
En un portal se oculta.
Un soneto buscaba
Perdido entre sus plumas.

La palabra esperada
Ilumina los ámbitos;
Un nuevo amor resurge
Al sentido postrado.

Olvidados los sueños
Los aires se los llevan.
Reposo. Convertida
La ternura se deja.

X

Love moves the world
That lies at rest,
Lost to sight. And this
Tenderness not bound to service.

The lights undertake
Their daily exodus
Through the streets, leaving
Space empty and quiet.

And the angel appears;
He hides in a doorway.
He was looking for a lost
Sonnet in his plumes.

The long-awaited word
Illumines atmospheres;
A new love revives
Declining senses.

Forgotten dreams
Are carried off by the air.
Repose. Tenderness,
Transformed, lets go.

REMORDIMIENTO EN TRAJE DE NOCHE

Un hombre gris avanza por la calle de niebla;
No lo sospecha nadie. Es un cuerpo vacío;
Vacío como pampa, como mar, como viento,
Desiertos tan amargos bajo un cielo implacable.

Es el tiempo pasado, y sus alas ahora
Entre la sombra encuentran una pálida fuerza;
Es el remordimiento, que de noche, dudando,
En secreto aproxima su sombra descuidada.

No estrechéis esa mano. La yedra altivamente
Ascenderá cubriendo los troncos del invierno.
Invisible en la calma el hombre gris camina.
¿No sentís a los muertos? Mas la tierra está sorda.

REMORSE IN BLACK TIE

A gray man walks the foggy street.
No one suspects. An empty body,
Empty as plains or sea or wind:
Harsh deserts under unrelenting sky.

It is the past, and now his wings
In shadow meet a pallid force;
Thus hesitant remorse, at night,
Brings near its heedless shadow secretly.

Don't take that hand! The prideful ivy
Will rise about the boles of winter.
In calm, the gray man goes unseen.
Do you not hear the dead? But earth is deaf.

CUERPO EN PENA

Lentamente el ahogado recorre sus dominios
Donde el silencio quita su apariencia a la vida.
Transparentes llanuras inmóviles le ofrecen
Árboles sin colores y pájaros callados.

Las sombras indecisas alargándose tiemblan,
Mas el viento no mueve sus alas irisadas;
Si el ahogado sacude sus lívidos recuerdos,
Halla un golpe de luz, la memoria del aire.

Un vidrio denso tiembla delante de las cosas,
Un vidrio que despierta formas color de olvido;
Olvidos de tristeza, de un amor, de la vida,
Ahogados como un cuerpo sin luz, sin aire, muerto.

Delicados, con prisa, se insinúan apenas
Vagos revuelos grises, encendiendo en el agua
Reflejos de metal o aceros relucientes,
Y su rumbo acuchilla las simétricas olas.

Flores de luz tranquila despiertan a lo lejos,
Flores de luz quizá, o miradas tan bellas
Como pudo el ahogado soñarlas una noche,
Sin amor ni dolor, en su tumba infinita.

A su fulgor el agua seducida se aquieta,
Azulada sonrisa asomando en sus ondas.
Sonrisas, oh miradas alegres de los labios;
Miradas, oh sonrisas de la luz triunfante.

BODY IN TORMENT

Where silence deadens life's appearance
The drowned man views his new domain:
Transparent, motionless plains display
Trees without color and quiet birds.

Irresolute shadows tremble lengthening,
But here the rainbowed wings of the wind
Are still, and if he shakes his livid memories
He finds a stroke of light — the remembrance of air.

In front of things, a thick glass trembles,
Glass that rouses forms the color of oblivion,
All sadness, love, and life, forgotten, drowned
As a body without light or air now, dead.

A vague and rapid turbulence appears,
Delicate and gray, kindling in water
Reflections of metal or shining blades
Whose course runs through the symmetry of waves.

Distant blooms of tranquil light awaken,
Blossoms of light, perhaps, or such sweet glances
As the drowned man was able to dream one night,
Loveless, painless, lost in his infinite tomb.

In their brilliance the charmed water grows calm,
And a blue smile appears in the waves.
Those smiles — the lips' happy glances!
The glances — smiles of light triumphant!

Desdobla sus espejos la prisión delicada;
Claridad sinuosa, errantes perspectivas.
Perspectivas que rompe con su dolor ya muerto
Ese pálido rostro que solemne aparece.

Su insomnio maquinal el ahogado pasea.
El silencio impasible sonríe en sus oídos.
Inestable vacío sin alba ni crepúsculo.
Monótona tristeza, emoción en ruinas.

En plena mar al fin, sin rumbo, a toda vela;
Hacia lo lejos, más, hacia la flor sin nombre.
Atravesar ligero como pájaro herido
Ese cristal confuso, esas luces extrañas.

Pálido entre las ondas cada vez más opacas
El ahogado ligero se pierde ciegamente
En el fondo nocturno como un astro apagado.
Hacia lo lejos, sí, hacia el aire sin nombre.

A River, A Love

The tenuous prison multiplies its mirrors,
A sinuous clarity, drifting scenes.
Perspectives that the pallid face, its pain
Dead now, breaks through, appearing solemnly.

Insomniac automaton, he strolls,
While in his ears, unfeeling silence grins.
Unstable void with neither dawn nor dusk,
Monotonous sadness, and emotion ruined.

At last, high seas, no course, full sail;
Toward the distance, and beyond, the nameless flower.
Like an injured bird, to cross, go through
That clouded, difficult crystal, those strange lights.

In waters growing dark, the drowned man goes
Pale and floating lightly, blindly lost
In nocturnal depths, a star come down and quenched,
Toward the distance, yes, toward nameless air.

DESTIERRO

Ante las puertas bien cerradas,
Sobre un río de olvido, va la canción antigua.
Una luz lejos piensa
Como a través de un cielo.
Todos acaso duermen,
Mientras él lleva su destino a solas.

Fatiga de estar vivo, de estar muerto,
Con frío en vez de sangre,
Con frío que sonríe insinuando
Por las aceras apagadas.

Le abandona la noche y la aurora lo encuentra,
Tras sus huellas la sombra tenazmente.

EXILE

Past all the shuttered doors
Along a river of oblivion, the old song runs.
The light in the distance
Meditates as if through the sky.
Perhaps they are all asleep;
And he bears his lot alone.

A weariness of living and dying,
With cold in the veins instead of blood,
Cold that insinuates and grins
Down the dull sidewalks.

He is abandoned by darkness, and dawn finds him;
Tracking him down, his shadow stubbornly.

DESDICHA

Un día comprendió cómo sus brazos eran
Solamente de nubes;
Imposible con nubes estrechar hasta el fondo
Un cuerpo, una fortuna.

La fortuna es redonda y cuenta lentamente
Estrellas del estío.
Hacen falta unos brazos seguros como el viento,
Y como el mar un beso.

Pero él con sus labios,
Con sus labios no sabe sino decir palabras;
Palabras hacia el techo,
Palabras hacia el suelo,
Y sus brazos son nubes que transforman la vida
En aire navegable.

MISFORTUNE

One day he understood in what way his arms were
Merely clouds —
Impossible to clasp a body tightly,
Or fortune, with clouds.

Fortune is round and slowly counts
The summer stars.
He needs arms as certain as the wind,
And a kiss like the sea.

But he, with his lips,
He can do nothing with his lips but speak words,
Words to the ceiling
Words to the floor.
And his arms are clouds that change life
To navigable air.

DUERME, MUCHACHO

La rabia de la muerte, los cuerpos torturados,
La revolución, abanico en la mano,
Impotencia del poderoso, hambre del sediento,
Duda con manos de duda y pies de duda;

La tristeza, agitando sus collares
Para alegrar un poco tantos viejos;
Todo unido entre tumbas como estrellas,
Entre lujurias como lunas;

La muerte, la pasión en los cabellos,
Dormitan tan minúsculas como un árbol,
Dormitan tan pequeñas o tan grandes
Como un árbol crecido hasta llegar al suelo.

Hoy sin embargo está también cansado.

SLEEP, CHILD

Death's fury, tortured bodies,
Revolution, while hands hold open fans,
The impotence of the powerful and the hunger of the
       thirsting,
Doubt, with hands of doubt and feet of doubt;

Sadness, shaking its necklaces
To enliven a little all the old;
All one among tombs like stars,
And moonlike lubricities;

As tiny as a tree,
Death and these passionate tresses
Now begin to nod, to doze as tiny or as tall
As a tree grown all the way to the ground.

But today he too is tired.

DRAMA O PUERTA CERRADA

La juventud sin escolta de nubes,
Los muros, voluntad de tempestades,
La lámpara, como abanico fuera o dentro,
Dicen con eloquencia aquello no ignorado,
Aquello que algún día débilmente
Ante la muerte misma se abandona.

Hueso aplastado por la piedra de sueños,
¿Qué hacer, desprovistos de salida,
Si no es sobre puente tendido por el rayo
Para unir dos mentiras,
Mentira de vivir o mentira de carne?

Sólo sabemos esculpir biografías
En músicas hostiles;
Sólo sabemos contar afirmaciones
O negaciones, cabellera de noche;
Sólo sabemos invocar como niños al frío
Por miedo de irnos solos a la sombra del tiempo.

DRAMA, OR A CLOSED DOOR

Youth with no escort of clouds,
Walls, what the storms will,
The lamp, outside, like a fan, or in,
With eloquence all declare the obvious:
That which one day weakly gives
Itself over, yes, to death.

Bone crushed by the stone of dreams,
What to do — denied escape —
If not on the bridge that leaps with a flash of light
Between two lies —
The lie of life, or the lie of the flesh?

We know so little! — how to sculpt
Biographies in hostile music;
How to count up affirmations
Or denials, the night's long hair;
How like children to invoke the cold
For fear of going alone into the shadow of time.

NOCTURNO ENTRE LAS MUSARAÑAS

Cuerpo de piedra, cuerpo triste,
Entre lanas como muros de universo,
Idéntico a las razas cuando cumplen años,
A los más inocentes edificios,
A las más pudorosas cataratas,
Blancas como la noche, en tanto la montaña
Despedaza formas enloquecidas,
Despedaza dolores como dedos,
Alegrías como uñas.

No saber donde ir, donde volver,
Buscando los vientos piadosos
Que destruyen las arrugas del mundo,
Que bendicen los deseos cortados a raíz
Antes de dar su flor,
Su flor grande como un niño.

Los labios quieren esa flor
Cuyo puño, besado por la noche,
Abre las puertas del olvido labio a labio.

NOCTURNE AMONG GROTESQUERIES

Body of stone, morose body
In woolens like the walls of the universe,
Body like the birthdays of the races,
Like edifices overwhelmingly innocent,
Like the shyest waterfalls
White as the night, while the mountain
Rips up manic shapes,
Pains like fingers
And pleasures like fingernails.

Not knowing where to go, where to go back to,
Seeking those merciful winds
That wear away the wrinkles in the earth,
That bless those desires cut out at the roots
Before flowering.
Their great blossom, like a child.

Lips want that flower
Whose fist, kissed by the night,
Opens the doors of oblivion lip by lip.

115063

DIRÉ CÓMO NACISTEIS

Diré cómo nacisteis, placeres prohibidos,
Como nace un deseo sobre torres de espanto,
Amenazadores barrotes, hiel descolorida,
Noche petrificada a fuerza de puños,
Ante todos, incluso el más rebelde,
Apto solamente en la vida sin muros.

Corazas infranqueables, lanzas o puñales,
Todo es bueno si deforma un cuerpo;
Tu deseo es beber esas hojas lascivas
O dormir en ese agua acariciadora.
No importa;
Ya declaran tu espíritu impuro.

No importa la pureza, los dones que un destino
Levantó hacia las aves con manos imperecederas;
No importa la juventud, sueño más que hombre,
La sonrisa tan noble, playa de seda bajo la tempestad
De un régimen caído.

Placeres prohibidos, planetas terrenales,
Miembros de mármol con sabor de estío,
Jugo de esponjas abandonadas por el mar,
Flores de hierro, resonantes como el pecho de un
        hombre.

I WILL TELL HOW YOU WERE BORN

I will tell how you were born, forbidden pleasures:
As desire is born over towers of fear,
The threatening bars, discolored bile,
The night petrified by fists,
In front of everyone, even the rebel
Who will not live within walls.

Impenetrable armor, spears or daggers,
Everything that deforms the body is good;
What you want is to drink those lascivious leaves
Or to sleep in that caressing water.
It's not important:
Already they declare your spirit impure.

But purity is not important, the gifts
That a fate of sorts lifted with unaging hands
Toward the birds in flight;
Youth is not important, more a dream than a man,
Such a noble smile, a silken beach beneath the storm
Of a fallen regime.

Forbidden pleasures, whole planets on earth!
Marble members with the taste of summer,
The life-juice of sponges abandoned by the sea,
Iron blossoms, resounding like the torso of a man.

Soledades altivas, coronas derribadas,
Libertades memorables, manto de juventudes;
Quien insulta esos frutos, tinieblas en la lengua,
Es vil como un rey, como sombra de rey
Arrastrándose a los pies de la tierra
Para conseguir un trozo de vida.

No sabía los límites impuestos,
Límites de metal o papel,
Ya que el azar le hizo abrir los ojos bajo una luz tan alta,
Adonde no llegan realidades vacías,
Leyes hediondas, códigos, ratas de paisajes derruidos.

Extender entonces la mano
Es hallar una montaña que prohibe,
Un bosque impenetrable que niega,
Un mar que traga adolescentes rebeldes.

Pero si la ira, el ultraje, el oprobio y la muerte,
Ávidos dientes sin carne todavía,
Amenazan abriendo sus torrentes,
De otro lado vosotros, placeres prohibidos,
Bronce de orgullo, blasfemia que nada precipita,
Tendéis en una mano el misterio,
Sabor que ninguna amargura corrompe,
Cielos, cielos relampagueantes que aniquilan.

Abajo, estatuas anónimas,
Sombras de sombras, miseria, preceptos de niebla;
Una chispa de aquellos placeres
Brilla en la hora vengativa.
Su fulgor puede destruir vuestro mundo.

Forbidden Pleasures

Haughty solitudes, toppled crowns,
Memorable liberties, mantle of youth —
Whoever insults these fruits, a darkness on the tongue,
Is as wretched as a king, as the shadow of a king
Groveling at the heels of the earth
For a little slice of life.

He did not know the imposed limits
Of metal or paper,
When mere chance opened his eyes by force
Beneath so lofty a light,
Where empty realities cannot reach —
The stinking laws, codes, rats from ruined regions.

To reach out now
Is to touch a forbidding mountain,
An impenetrable forest that denies,
An ocean swallowing rebellious youths.

But if anger, outrage, condemnation and death —
Eager fangs awaiting flesh —
Threaten you in a torrent,
Then, forbidden pleasures,
Proud bronze, gratuitous blasphemy,
In one hand you hold the mystery,
The taste no bitterness can taint,
Skies, electric heavens that annihilate!

Down with the anonymous statues,
Shadows of shadows, poverty, foggy precepts.
A spark of those pleasures
Shines in the hour of vengeance!
Its brilliance can destroy your world.

TELARAÑAS CUELGAN DE LA RAZÓN

Telarañas cuelgan de la razón
En un paisaje de ceniza absorta;
Ha pasado el huracán de amor,
Ya ningún pájaro queda.

Tampoco ninguna hoja,
Todas van lejos, como gotas de agua
De un mar cuando se seca,
Cuando no hay ya lágrimas bastantes,
Porque alguien, cruel como un día de sol en primavera,
Con su sola presencia ha dividido en dos un cuerpo.

Ahora hace falta recoger los trozos de prudencia,
Aunque siempre nos falte alguno;
Recoger la vida vacía
Y caminar esperando que lentamente se llene,
Si es posible, otra vez, como antes,
De sueños desconocidos y deseos invisibles.

Tú nada sabes de ello,
Tú estás allá, cruel como el día;
El día, esa luz que abraza estrechamente un triste muro,
Un muro, ¿no comprendes?
Un muro frente al cual estoy solo.

THE MIND IS HUNG WITH COBWEBS

The mind is hung with cobwebs
In a landscape of astonished ash;
Love's hurricane has passed overhead:
Not a bird left.

Nor a leaf.
They disappear like drops of water
When an ocean goes dry.
When tears are not enough
Because as cruel as a spring day of sun someone
Splits a body in two with his mere presence.

Now we need to gather up the pieces of prudence,
Though one of them is always missing,
To collect this empty life
And go along hoping it will slowly fill up
If possible, again, as before
With unrecognized dreams and invisible desires.

Oh you know nothing of this,
You are over there, as cruel as the day,
The day, the light that tightly holds some sorrowful wall.
A wall — can't you understand?
A wall I face alone.

NO DECÍA PALABRAS

No decía palabras,
Acercaba tan sólo un cuerpo interrogante,
Porque ignoraba que el deseo es una pregunta
Cuya respuesta no existe,
Una hoja cuya rama no existe,
Un mundo cuyo cielo no existe.

La angustia se abre paso entre los huesos,
Remonta por las venas
Hasta abrirse en la piel,
Surtidores de sueño
Hechos carne en interrogación vuelta a las nubes.

Un roce al paso,
Una mirada fugaz entre las sombras,
Bastan para que el cuerpo se abra en dos,
Ávido de recibir en sí mismo
Otro cuerpo que sueñe;
Mitad y mitad, sueño y sueño, carne y carne,
Iguales en figura, iguales en amor, iguales en deseo.

Aunque sólo sea una esperanza,
Porque el deseo es una pregunta cuya respuesta nadie
    sabe.

HE DID NOT SPEAK WORDS

He did not speak words
Merely drew near
     An inquisitive body
Not knowing that desire is a question
Whose answer does not exist
A leaf whose branch does not exist
A world beneath a nonexistent sky.

Anguish makes its way through the bones
Rises up along the veins
Until it breaks the skin
Fountains of dream made flesh
And questioning the clouds.

A light touch in passing
A quick glance into the shadows
Are enough for the body to split in two,
Greedy to take in
Another dreaming body
Half to half, dream and dream, flesh and flesh,
Alike in form, alike in love, equal in desire.

Even if this were only a wish —
For desire is a question whose answer is unknown.

UNOS CUERPOS SON COMO FLORES

Unos cuerpos son como flores,
Otros como puñales,
Otros como cintas de agua;
Pero todos, temprano o tarde,
Serán quemaduras que en otro cuerpo se agranden,
Convirtiendo por virtud del fuego a una piedra en un
      hombre.

Pero el hombre se agita en todas direcciones,
Sueña con libertades, compite con el viento,
Hasta que un día la quemadura se borra,
Volviendo a ser piedra en el camino de nadie.

Yo, que no soy piedra, sino camino
Que cruzan al pasar los pies desnudos,
Muero de amor por todos ellos;
Les doy mi cuerpo para que lo pisen,
Aunque les lleve a una ambición o a una nube,
Sin que ninguno comprenda
Que ambiciones o nubes
No valen un amor que se entrega.

BODIES LIKE FLOWERS

Some have bodies like flowers,
Others, like knives,
And others, like ribbons of water;
But sooner or later they will all
Be deep burns deepening in another's body,
By fire changing a stone into a man.

But man, trembling, starts in all directions,
Dreams of liberties, vies with the wind,
Until one day the burn heals
And again he lies like a stone in a path no one walks.

I am not a stone, but a path
Trodden by naked, passing feet;
I die of a love for them all;
My body is given them to tread
Though it lead them to ambition or a cloud,
And none of them sees
That neither ambition nor cloud
Is worth love offered openly.

PASIÓN POR PASIÓN

Pasión por pasión. Amor por amor.

Estaba en una calle de ceniza, limitada por vastos edificios de arena. Allí encontré al placer. Le miré: en sus ojos vacíos había dos relojes pequeños; uno marchaba en sentido contrario al otro. En la comisura de los labios sostenía una flor mordida. Sobre los hombros llevaba una capa en jirones.

A su paso unas estrellas se apagaban, otras se encendían. Quise detenerle; mi brazo quedó inmóvil. Lloré, lloré tanto, que hubiera podido llenar sus órbitas vacías. Entonces amaneció.

Comprendí por qué llaman prudente a un hombre sin cabeza.

PASSION FOR PASSION

Passion for passion. Love for love.

I was in a street of ash, lined with huge buildings of sand. I found pleasure there. I looked at him: in his empty eyes there were two tiny clocks; they ran in opposite directions. He held a flower in the corner of his mouth, bitten and broken. The cape on his shoulders was in shreds.

As he passed, some stars began to die, others were being born. I tried to stop him. My arms hung motionless. I wept. I wept so much I could have filled his empty orbits. Then it was dawn.

I understood why a man is called prudent when headless.

COMO LEVE SONIDO

Como leve sonido:
Hoja que roza un vidrio,
Agua que pasa unas guijas,
Lluvia que besa una frente juvenil;

Como rápida caricia:
Pie desnudo sobre el camino,
Dedos que ensayan el primer amor,
Sábanas tibias sobre el cuerpo solitario;

Como fugaz deseo:
Seda brillante en la luz,
Esbelto adolescente entrevisto,
Lágrimas por ser más que un hombre;

Como esta vida que no es mía
Y sin embargo es la mía,
Como este afán sin nombre
Que no me pertenece y sin embargo soy yo;

Como todo aquello que de cerca o de lejos
Me roza, me besa, me hiere,
Tu presencia está conmigo fuera y dentro,
Es mi vida misma y no es mi vida,
Así como una hoja y otra hoja
Son la apariencia del viento que las lleva.

LIKE A FAINT SOUND

Like a faint sound:
A leaf brushing glass,
Water over pebbles,
Kiss of rain on a young forehead;

Like a quick caress:
Naked foot on the path,
Fingers that give love a first try,
Warm sheets over a solitary body;

Like a sudden, swift desire:
Silk shining in the light,
Slim youth only glimpsed,
Tears, for being more than a man;

Like this life that is not mine
And yet is mine,
Like this nameless eagerness
That does not belong to me and yet is me;

Like everything close by or far away
That brushes against me, kisses me, wounds me,
Your presence is within me and without,
Is my life itself and is not my life,
Just as one leaf, and another,
Become the mere appearance of the wind.

II

Como una vela sobre el mar
Resume ese azulado afán que se levanta
Hasta las estrellas futuras,
Hecho escala de olas
Por donde pies divinos descienden al abismo,
También tu forma misma,
Ángel, demonio, sueño de un amor soñado,
Resume en mí un afán que en otro tiempo levantaba
Hasta las nubes sus olas melancólicas.

Sintiendo todavía los pulsos de ese afán,
Yo, el más enamorado,
En las orillas del amor,
Sin que una luz me vea
Definitivamente muerto o vivo,
Contemplo sus olas y quisiera anegarme,
Deseando perdidamente
Descender, como los ángeles aquellos por la escala de
    espuma,
Hasta el fondo del mismo amor que ningún hombre ha
    visto.

II

Like one sail at sea,
Concentrating all that blue longing
That rises toward future stars
As a staircase of waves
Where divine feet descend to the abyss,
So you are the figure —
You angel, demon, dream of a dreamed love —
Concentrating in me the longing
That once lifted sorrowful waves toward the clouds.

Still shuddering with that longing,
Without the light that would
Reveal me clearly dead or alive,
I, the most enamored, on love's shore
Stare at the waves and want to sink in them
Like those angels; I must descend
The ladder of foam
Despondently, to love-depths that no man has seen!

VI

El mar es un olvido
Una canción, un labio;
El mar es un amante,
Fiel respuesta al deseo.

Es como un ruiseñor,
Y sus aguas son plumas,
Impulsos que levantan
A las frías estrellas.

Sus caricias son sueño,
Entreabren la muerte,
Son lunas accesibles,
Son la vida más alta.

Sobre espaldas oscuras
Las olas van gozando.

VI

The sea is an oblivion,
A song, one lip;
The sea is a lover,
Faithful answer to desire.

It is like a nightingale,
And its waters are feathers,
Impulses which rise
To the cold stars.

Its caresses are sleep,
They half-open death,
They are attainable moons,
They are the highest life.

Over dark backs
The waves slide in pleasure.

VII

Adolescente fui en días idénticos a nubes.
Cosa grácil, visible por penumbra y reflejo,
Y extraño es, si ese recuerdo busco,
Que tanto, tanto duela sobre el cuerpo de hoy.

Perder placer es triste
Como la dulce lámpara sobre el lento nocturno;
Aquél fui, aquél fui, aquél he sido;
Era la ignorancia mi sombra.

Ni gozo ni pena; fui niño
Prisionero entre muros cambiantes;
Historias como cuerpos, cristales como cielos,
Sueño luego, un sueño más alto que la vida.

Cuando la muerte quiera
Una verdad quitar de entre mis manos,
Las hallará vacías, como en la adolescencia
Ardientes de deseo, tendidas hacia el aire.

VII

I was young when the days were like clouds,
A slender thing, seen in darkness or reflection,
And if I seek that memory now, it strangely
Pains this body of today.

How sad to lose pleasure!
Like a gentle lamp in the languid night.
That one was I, that one was I, thus I have been;
And ignorance was my shadow.

Neither pleasure nor pain; I was a child
Imprisoned in shifting walls,
Histories like the body, windows like sky,
Then sleep, a dream higher than life.

When death resolves
To rob my hands of some truth,
It will find them empty. As in youth
They will burn with desire, held empty in the air.

LA GLORIA DEL POETA

Demonio hermano mío, mi semejante,
Te vi palidecer, colgado como la luna matinal,
Oculto en una nube por el cielo,
Entre las horribles montañas,
Una llama a guisa de flor tras la menuda oreja tentadora,
Blasfemando lleno de dicha ignorante,
Igual que un niño cuando entona su plegaria,
Y burlándote cruelmente al contemplar mi cansancio de
　　la tierra.

Mas no eres tú,
Amor mío hecho eternidad,
Quien deba reír de este sueño, de esta impotencia, de
　　esta caída,
Porque somos chispas de un mismo fuego
Y un mismo soplo nos lanzó sobre las ondas tenebrosas
De una extraña creación, donde los hombres
Se acaban como un fósforo al trepar los fatigosos años
　　de sus vidas.

Tu carne como la mía
Desea tras el agua y el sol el roce de la sombra;
Nuestra palabra anhela
El muchacho semejante a una rama florida
Que pliega la gracia de su aroma y color en el aire cálido
　　de mayo;
Nuestros ojos el mar monótono y diverso,
Poblado por el grito de las aves grises en la tormenta,
Nuestra mano hermosos versos que arrojar al desdén de
　　los hombres.

THE POET'S GLORY

Demon brother mine, *mon semblable*,
I saw you blanch, suspended like the morning moon
Hidden in a cloud
Between horrible mountains! —
With a flame like a blossom behind your enticing little
    ear —
Blaspheming and full of ignorant bliss
Like a child intoning its prayers,
And gibing cruelly at my weariness of this earth.

But my immortal love, it is not you
Who should be laughing at this dream, this impotence,
    this fall —
You and I are sparks of the same flame!
And the same breath cast us out over the dark waves
Of a strange creation, where men
Go out like matches as they trudge down the deadening
Years of their lives.

Like mine, your flesh
Desires — after water and sun — the touch of shadow;
Our word passionately
Wants the youth like a flowering branch
Who plaits his loveliness of scent and hue in the warm
    spring air;
Our eyes want the monotonous, diverse sea,
Filled with the gray birds' cries in the storm;
Our hands want lovely verses to scatter to the disdain of
    men.

63

Los hombres tú los conoces, hermano mío;
Mírales cómo enderezan su invisible corona
Mientras se borran en la sombra con sus mujeres al
    brazo,
Carga de suficiencia inconsciente,
Llevando a comedida distancia del pecho,
Como sacerdotes católicos la forma de su triste dios,
Los hijos conseguidos en unos minutos que se hurtaron
    al sueño
Para dedicarlos a la cohabitación, en la densa tiniebla
    conyugal
De sus cubiles, escalonados los unos sobre los otros.

Mírales perdidos en la naturaleza,
Cómo enferman entre los graciosos castaños o los
    taciturnos plátanos.
Cómo levantan con avaricia el mentón,
Sintiendo un miedo oscuro morderles los talones;
Mira cómo desertan de su trabajo el séptimo día
    autorizado,
Mientras la caja, el mostrador, la clínica, el bufete, el
    despacho oficial
Dejan pasar el aire con callado rumor por su ámbito
    solitario.

Escúchales brotar interminables palabras
Aromatizadas de facilidad violenta,
Reclamando un abrigo para el niño encadenado bajo el
    sol divino
O una bebida tibia, que resguarde aterciopeladamente
El clima de sus fauces,
A quienes dañaría la excesiva frialdad del agua natural.

Ah you know men well, my brother —
See how they straighten their invisible crowns
As they fade into the shadows
With their wives on their arms
(Freight of unconscious sufficiency!)
And see how they carry —
At a proper arm's length,
As Catholic priests carry the figure of their dreary god —
The children gotten in the few minutes
Stolen from sleep and dedicated to intercourse
In the deep conjugal darkness
Of their lairs, clambering on top of one another.

Look at them!
Lost in nature, among the lovely chestnut trees
Or reticent plane-trees, how they sicken!
How they set their chins with avarice
As they feel a dark fear nipping at their heels.
See them desert their work
On the allotted seventh day,
And then cashbox, counter, clinic, desk and office
Let the air flow through their solitary domain
In silence.

Listen to them spout endless words
Perfumed with violent ease:
They want an overcoat for the child chained in the
        divine sunlight,
Or a tepid drink, to sooth — oh so gently —
The clime of their own gullets,
Whom cool tapwater would harm.

65

Oye sus marmóreos preceptos
Sobre lo útil, lo normal y lo hermoso;
Óyeles dictar la ley al mundo, acotar el amor, dar canon
    a la belleza inexpresable,
Mientras deleitan sus sentidos con altavoces delirantes;
Contempla sus extraños cerebros
Intentando levantar, hijo a hijo, un complicado edificio
    de arena
Que negase con torva frente lívida la refulgente paz de
    las estrellas.

Ésos son, hermano mío,
Los seres con quienes muero a solas,
Fantasmas que harán brotar un día
El solemne erudito, oráculo de estas palabras mías ante
    alumnos extraños,
Obteniendo por ello renombre,
Más una pequeña casa de campo en la angustiosa sierra
    inmediata a la capital;
En tanto tú, tras irisada niebla,
Acaricias los rizos de tu cabellera
Y contemplas con gesto distraído desde la altura
Esta sucia tierra donde el poeta se ahoga.

Listen to their marmoreal precepts
On the useful, the normal, the beautiful;
Listen to them dictate law to the world, fix the norms
of love, give rules for ineffable beauty,
While they delight their senses with delirious
loudspeakers;
Contemplate their strange minds,
Attempting to raise, son by son, a complex edifice of sand
Whose grim, livid facade would negate the refulgent
peace of the stars.

These, my brother,
Surround my solitary dying —
Specters that someday will spawn
The solemn scholar, the oracle
Who will display my words for alien students,
And therewith gaining renown,
Get a little country place in the tortuous mountains
Near the capital.
While behind your rainbow fog
You stroke your curly hair
And from the heights distractedly contemplate
This filthy earth where the poet slowly suffocates.

Sabes sin embargo que mi voz es la tuya,
Que mi amor es el tuyo;
Deja, oh, deja por una larga noche
Resbalar tu cálido cuerpo oscuro,
Ligero como un látigo,
Bajo el mío, momia de hastío sepulta en anónima
      yacija,
Y que tus besos, ese venero inagotable,
Viertan en mí la fiebre de una pasión a muerte entre
      los dos;
Porque me cansa la vana tarea de las palabras,
Como al niño las dulces piedrecillas
Que arroja a un lago, para ver estremecerse su calma
Con el reflejo de una gran ala misteriosa.

Es hora ya, es más que tiempo
De que tus manos cedan a mi vida
El amargo puñal codiciado del poeta;
De que lo hundas, con sólo un golpe limpio,
En este pecho sonoro y vibrante, idéntico a un laúd,
Donde la muerte únicamente,
La muerte únicamente,
Puede hacer resonar la melodía prometida.

But you know that my voice is yours,
And my love.
Please, please for one long night
Let your burnished body
Slip as quick as a whip beneath mine,
Beneath this mummy of ennui interred in a forgotten
       tomb . . .
And let your limitless fountain of kisses
Spill in me the fever of a passion unto death between us!
This useless work of words tires me
The way sweet pebbles tire the child who throws them
       into a pond
To see the calm shattered
By the reflection of a great, mysterious wing.

It is time now, and long overdue,
For your hands to give my life
The bitter dagger. It is what the poet covets.
Time for you to sink it with one clean blow
Into this breast, as sonorous and vibrant as a lute,
Where only death,
Only death
Can pluck the promised melody.

A LAS ESTATUAS DE LOS DIOSES

Hermosas y vencidas soñáis,
Vueltos los ciegos ojos hacia el cielo,
Mirando las remotas edades
De titánicos hombres,
Cuyo amor os daba ligeras guirnaldas
Y la olorosa llama se alzaba
Hacia la luz divina, su hermana celeste.

Reflejo de vuestra verdad, las criaturas
Adictas y libres como el agua iban;
Aún no había mordido la brillante maldad
Sus cuerpos llenos de majestad y gracia.
En vosotros creían y vosotros existíais;
La vida no era un delirio sombrío.

La miseria y las muerte futuras,
No pensadas aún, en vuestras manos
Bajo un inofensivo sueño adormecían
Sus venenosas flores bellas,
Y una y otra vez el mismo amor tornaba
Al pecho de los hombres,
Como ave fiel que vuelve al nido
Cuando el día, entre las altas ramas,
Con apacible risa va entornando los ojos.

Eran tiempos heroicos y frágiles,
Deshechos con vuestro poder como un sueño feliz.
Hoy yacéis, mutiladas y oscuras,
Entre los grises jardines de las ciudades,
Piedra inútil que el soplo celeste no anima,
Abandonadas de la súplica y la humana esperanza.

TO THE STATUES OF THE GODS

Beautiful and beaten, you sleep,
Blind eyes turned toward the sky,
Where you see the remote epochs
Of titanic men,
Whose devotion gave you light garlands,
And the aromatic flame rose
Toward the divine light, its celestial sister.

The reflection of your truth, all creatures
Moved as captive and free as water;
Brilliant evil had not yet eaten at
Their majestic, graceful bodies.
They believed in you, and you existed;
Life was not then a delirium in darkness.

Future wretchedness and death,
Not yet conceived, in your hands
Lulled their lovely venomous flowers
In a harmless doze,
And once and again love itself
Came back to the breast of man
Like a faithful bird that returns to the nest
When daylight, through high branches,
Draws its eyelids shut with gentle laughter.

Those were heroic, fragile times —
Shattered, along with your power, like a sweet dream.
Now you lie mutilated and obscure
Among the gray gardens of cities,
Useless stone which no celestial breeze enlivens,
Abandoned by human hopes and supplication.

La lluvia con la luz resbalan
Sobre tanta muerte memorable,
Mientras desfilan a lo lejos muchedumbres
Que antaño impíamente desertaron
Vuestros marmóreos altares,
Santificados en la memoria del poeta.

Tal vez su fe os devuelva el cielo.
Mas no juzguéis por el rayo, la guerra o la plaga
Una triste humanidad decaída;
Impasibles reinad en el divino espacio.
Distraiga con su gracia el copero solícito
La cólera de vuestro poder que despierta.

En tanto el poeta, en la noche otoñal,
Bajo el blanco embeleso lunático,
Mira las ramas que el verdor abandona
Nevarse de luz beatamente,
Y sueña con vuestro trono de oro
Y vuestra faz cegadora,
Lejos de los hombres,
Allá en la altura impenetrable.

Invocations

Rain and light wash over
So much memorable death,
While in the distance the crowds
Who once impiously deserted
Your marble altars — still
Holy in the poet's memory — file past.

Perhaps it is his faith that will return
The heavens to you. But do not send thunderbolts,
War, or plague, in judgment on this sorrowful,
Decayed mankind; reign impassive in divine space.
Let the solicitous cupbearer, with his grace,
Distract the rage of your awakening powers.

While the poet, in the autumn night,
Under the moon's white rapture,
Watches the branches abandoned by green
Grow snowy with blessed light,
And the dreams of the golden throne,
And the blinding countenance,
Far from men,
Away in the impenetrable heavens.

A UN POETA MUERTO
(F. G. L.)

Así como en la roca nunca vemos
La clara flor abrirse,
Entre un pueblo hosco y duro
No brilla hermosamente
El fresco y alto ornato de la vida.
Por esto te mataron, porque eras
Verdor en nuestra tierra árida
Y azul en nuestro oscuro aire.

Leve es la parte de la vida
Que como dioses rescatan los poetas.
El odio y destrucción perduran siempre
Sordamente en la entraña
Toda hiel sempiterna del español terrible,
Que acecha lo cimero
Con su piedra en la mano.

Triste sino nacer
Con algún don ilustre
Aquí, donde los hombres
En su miseria sólo saben
El insulto, la mofa, el recelo profundo
Ante aquel que ilumina las palabras opacas
Por el oculto fuego originario.

TO A DEAD POET
(F. G. L.)

Just as one never sees bright petals
Spring from rock,
Thus among a hard and sullen people
There is no proud new ornament of life
To flower in splendor.
For this they killed you;
You were the green in our barren land,
And the blue in our dark air.

It is only a fragment of life
That poets can ransom like gods.
Mute hatred and destruction always survive
In the perennially
Bilious guts of the terrible Spaniard
Who lies in wait for what is glorious
With a stone in his hand.

Here, to be born with a gift
Is misfortune;
Here men in their misery
Know only
Insults, scorn, and deep suspicion
Of anyone who illuminates opaque words
With the original, occult fire.

La sal de nuestro mundo eras,
Vivo estabas como un rayo de sol,
Y ya es tan sólo tu recuerdo
Quien yerra y pasa, acariciando
El muro de los cuerpos
Con el dejo de las adormideras
Que nuestros predecesores ingirieron
A orillas del olvido.

Si tu ángel acude a la memoria,
Sombras son estos hombres
Que aún palpitan tras las malezas de la tierra;
La muerte se diría
Más viva que la vida
Porque tu estás con ella,
Pasado el arco de su vasto imperio,
Poblándola de pájaros y hojas
Con tu gracia y tu juventud incomparables.

Aquí la primavera luce ahora.
Mira los radiantes mancebos
Que vivo tanto amaste
Efímeros pasar juntos al fulgor del mar.
Desnudos cuerpos bellos que se llevan
Tras de sí los deseos
Con su exquisita forma, y sólo encierran
Amargo zumo, que no alberga su espíritu
Un destello de amor ni de alto pensamiento.

You were the salt of our earth,
As alive as a ray of sunlight,
And now it is only your memory
That wanders and paces among us,
Caressing the wall of bodies,
With a trace of the poppies
Our predecessors imbibed
At the shores of oblivion.

If your angel hearkens to memory
Then these men who shudder still, hidden
In the underbrush, are mere shadows;
Death, one would say,
Is more alive than life —
Because you are there,
Beyond the portal of its enormous empire,
And with your youth, your incomparable grace,
You people it with birds and leaves.

Spring is radiant here now.
Look at the young men
Whom you loved when alive,
As they pass briefly beside the sea's deep glow.
Lovely bare bodies whose exquisite forms
Carry off desires, who conserve
Only a bitter sap, and in whose spirits there lodges
Not a flicker of love or lofty thought.

Igual todo prosigue,
Como entonces, tan mágico,
Que parece imposible
La sombra en que has caído.
Mas un inmenso afán oculto advierte
Que su ignoto aguijón tan sólo puede
Aplacarse en nosotros con la muerte
Como el afán del agua,
A quien no basta esculpirse en las olas,
Sino perderse anónima
En los limbos del mar.

Pero antes no sabías
La realidad más honda de este mundo:
El odio, el triste odio de los hombres,
Que en ti señalar quiso
Por el acero horrible su victoria,
Con tu angustia postrera
Bajo la luz tranquila de Granada,
Distante entre cipreses y laureles,
Y entre tus propias gentes
Y por las mismas manos
Que un día servilmente te halagaran.

The Clouds

Everything persists
As before, so bewitching
That the shadow you have fallen in
Seems impossible.
A vast, secret longing in us hints
That its incomprehensible sting
Can be salved only by death,
Like the longing of water
Which is not content to sculpt itself in waves,
But must lose itself
In an oceanic limbo.

But, in those days, you did not know
The most profound reality of this world:
Hatred, this miserable hatred among men
That had to prove its victory
In you, with its horrible blade,
With your final anguish
In the tranquil light of Granada,
Far off, among cypresses and laurels,
Among your own people
And by the same hands
That once offered you servile praise.

Para el poeta la muerte es la victoria;
Un viento demoníaco le impulsa por la vida,
Y si una fuerza ciega
Sin comprensión de amor
Transforma por un crimen
A ti, cantor, en héroe,
Contempla en cambio, hermano,
Cómo entre la tristeza y el desdén
Un poder más magnánimo permite a tus amigos
En un rincón pudrirse libremente.

Tenga tu sombra paz,
Busque otros valles,
Un río donde el viento
Se lleve los sonidos entre juncos
Y lirios y el encanto
Tan viejo de las aguas elocuentes,
En donde el eco como la gloria humana ruede,
Como ella de remoto,
Ajeno como ella y tan estéril.

Halle tu gran afán enajenado
El puro amor de un dios adolescente
Entre el verdor de las rosas eternas;
Porque este ansia divina, perdida aquí en la tierra,
Tras de tanto dolor y dejamiento,
Con su propia grandeza nos advierte
De alguna mente creadora inmensa,
Que concibe al poeta cual lengua de su gloria
Y luego le consuela a través de la muerte.

Death is a victory for the poet;
A demon wind drives him through life,
And if some blind force
Without love's understanding
Changes you from singer to hero
By its crime,
Then, my brother, consider
How among sadness and disdain
An even more magnanimous power permits your friends
To rot freely in some corner.

Peace to your shadow!
May it seek other valleys —
A river where the wind
Wafts the sounds through rushes
And lilies and the ancient spell
Of eloquent waters,
Where echoes revolve like human glory,
As distant, as foreign, and as sterile.

May your grand maddened longing
Find the pure love of a young god
Among green-leafed, eternal roses;
For that divine desire, now lost on earth
After so much grief and abandon,
Hints — with its own greatness —
Of some immense creating mind
Which conceives the poet as the voice of its own glory,
And will console him after death.

LAMENTO Y ESPERANZA

Soñábamos algunos cuando niños, caídos
En una vasta hora de ocio solitario
Bajo la lámpara, ante las estampas de un libro,
Con la revolución. Y vimos su ala fúlgida
Plegar como una mies los cuerpos poderosos.

Jóvenes luego, el sueño quedó lejos
De un mundo donde desorden e injusticia,
Hinchiendo oscuramente las ávidas ciudades,
Se alzaban hasta el aire absorto de los campos.
Y en la revolución pensábamos: un mar
Cuya ira azul tragase tanta fría miseria.

El hombre es una nube de la que el sueño es viento.
¿Quién podrá al pensamiento separarlo del sueño?
Sabedlo bien vosotros, los que envidiéis mañana
En la calma este soplo de muerte que nos lleva
Pisando entre ruinas un fango con rocío de sangre.

Un continente de mercaderes y de histriones,
Al acecho de este loco país, está esperando
Que vencido se hunda, solo ante su destino,
Para arrancar jirones de su esplendor antiguo.
Le alienta únicamente su propia gran historia dolorida.

LAMENTATION AND HOPE

When we were children, some of us, and deep
In an endless hour of solitude
Beneath the lamp, lost in a picture book,
We dreamed of revolution. We saw
Its resplendent wing reap like wheat
The bodies of the powerful.

Then the dream was left behind us, far
From a world where chaos and injustice
Stuffed the greedy cities with darkness
And rose into the astonished air of the fields.
And we thought of revolution: an ocean
To gorge in blue rage on so much cold misery.

A dream is the wind for the cloud that is man.
But who will finally separate thought from dream?
Know this well, you who tomorrow in a moment of calm
May welcome the gust of death
That shoves us onward through these ruins,
Treading on mud and slime wet with a blood-dew.

A continent of hucksters and buffoons,
Lying in ambush for this insane nation, waits
For it to sink, defeated and alone with its destiny,
So as to rip out the scraps of its old glory.
Only its dolorous history sustains it now.

Si con dolor el alma se ha templado, es invencible;
Pero, como el amor, debe el dolor ser mudo:
No lo digáis, sufridlo en esperanza. Así este pueblo iluso
Agonizará antes, presa ya de la muerte,
Y vedle luego abierto, rosa eterna en los mares.

If it is with grief that the soul is tempered,
It is invincible. But grief must be silent,
Like love. Do not speak — but suffer hopefully.
This deceived nation, now in agony as a prisoner
Of death, must open then on the waves as a deathless
     rose.

LA VISITA DE DIOS

Pasada se halla ahora la mitad de mi vida.
El cuerpo sigue en pie y las voces aún giran
Y resuenan con encanto marchito en mis oídos,
Mas los días esbeltos ya se marcharon lejos;
Sólo recuerdos pálidos de su amor me han dejado.
Como el labrador al ver su trabajo perdido
Vuelve al cielo los ojos esperando la lluvia,
También quiero esperar en esta hora confusa
Unas lágrimas divinas que aviven mi cosecha.

Pero hondamente fijo queda el desaliento,
Como huésped oscuro de mis sueños.
¿Puedo esperar acaso? Todo se ha dado al hombre
Tal distracción efímera de la existencia;
A nada puede unir este ansia suya que reclama
Una pausa de amor entre la fuga de las cosas.
Vano sería dolerse del trabajo, la casa, los amigos
        perdidos
En aquel gran negocio demoníaco de la guerra.

Estoy en la ciudad alzada para su orgullo por el rico,
Adonde la miseria oculta canta por las esquinas
O expone dibujos que me arrasan de lágrimas los ojos.
Y mordiendo mis puños con tristeza impotente
Aún cuento mentalmente mis monedas escasas,
Porque un trozo de pan aquí y unos vestidos
Suponen un esfuerzo mayor para lograrlos
Que el de los viejos héroes cuando vencían
Monstruos, rompiendo encantos con su lanza.

THE VISITATION OF GOD

Half my life is over. My body is still
On its feet, voices still revolve and echo
With fading charm around my head,
But the lissome days are far behind me now;
They have left me with only pale memories of love.
As the laborer who sees his work destroyed
Turns his eyes to the sky in hopes of rain,
I too want to await some godly tears
That might revive my harvest in this uncertain hour.

But dejection is deeply lodged,
Like a dark guest of my dreams.
Should I hope? Everything is given to man
As passing distraction from existence.
This longing of his, that calls for loving pause
In the flight of things, he can fasten to nothing.
Useless to complain of the work, and home,
And friends, now lost in the great demon commerce of
        war.

In this city raised by the rich for their own glory
Hidden misery sings on street corners
Or shows me sketches that fill my eyes with tears.
Biting my fists with impotent sadness
Mentally I recount my little money,
For here a crust of bread, a few clothes,
Presume a greater effort
Than that of the old heroes, conquerors
Of monsters, who shattered spells with a spear.

La revolución renance siempre, como un fénix
Llameante en el pecho de los desdichados.
Esto lo sabe el charlatán bajo los árboles
De las plazas, y su baba argentina, su cascabel sonoro,
Silbando entre las hojas, encanta al pueblo
Robusto y engañado con maligna elocuencia,
Y canciones de sangre acunan su miseria.

Por mi dolor comprendo que otros inmensos sufren
Hombres callados a quienes falta el ocio
Para arrojar al cielo su tormento. Mas no puedo
Copiar su enérgico silencio, que me alivia
Este consuelo de la voz, sin tierra y sin amigo,
En la profunda soledad de quien no tiene
Ya nada entre sus brazos, sino el aire en torno,
Lo mismo que un navío al alejarse sobre el mar.

¿Adónde han ido las viejas compañeras del hombre?
Mis zurcidoras de proyectos, mis tejedoras de esperanzas
Han muerto. Sus agujas y madejas reposan
Con polvo en un rincón, sin la melodía del trabajo.
Como una sombra aislada al filo de los días,
Voy repitiendo gestos y palabras mientras lejos escucho
El inmenso bostezo de los siglos pasados.

El tiempo, ese blanco desierto ilimitado,
Esa nada creadora, amenaza a los hombres
Y con luz inmortal se abre ante los deseos juveniles.
Unos quieren asir locamente su mágico reflejo,
Mas otros le conjuran con un hijo
Ofrecido en los brazos como víctima,
Porque de nueva vida se mantiene su vida
Como el agua del agua llorada por los hombres.

The Clouds

Revolution is always reborn,
Like a phoenix rising in flames from the bodies
Of the wretched. The charlatan standing under trees
In the square knows this: drooling silver, ringing his bell,
Whistling in the leaves, he charms
This hearty, gullible folk with malignant eloquence,
And lullabies of blood rock misery to sleep.

Through my own grief, I understand that others suffer
More than I, the silent ones who have no leisure
To hurl their tortured sufferings toward heaven.
But I cannot mimic their energetic silence;
Friendless, homeless, I am eased
By this solace of the voice,
In the deep solitude of one who has
Nothing in his arms but the air around him,
Like a ship that has steamed into landless seas.

Where have man's old consorts gone?
My weavers of plans, my spinners of hopes,
Are dead. Their needles and skeins lie
Heaped in a dusty corner, the work-song hushed.
Like a single shadow on the knife-edge of the days
I rehearse gestures and words, while far off I hear
The immense yawn of the centuries.

And time, that bare limitless desert,
That creating nothingness, threatens us
As it opens, with immortal light, before the desires
Of youth. Some insanely grasp at its magic shimmer,
But others conjure it with a child in their arms,
Offered as sacrifice —
For life feeds on new life,
As waters swell with lamentation.

Pero a ti, Dios, ¿con qué te aplacaremos?
Mi sed eras tú, tú fuiste mi amor perdido,
Mi casa rota, mi vida trabajada, y la casa y la vida
De tantos hombres como yo a la deriva
En el naufragio de un país. Levantados de naipes,
Uno tras otro iban cayendo mis pobres paraísos.
¿Movió tu mano el aire que fuera derribándolos
Y tras ellos, en el profundo abatimiento, en el hondo
      vacío,
Se alza al fin ante mí la nube que oculta tu presencia?

No golpees airado mi cuerpo con tu rayo;
Si el amor no eres tú, ¿quién lo será en tu mundo?
Compadécete al fin, escucha este murmullo
Que ascendiendo llega como una ola
Al pie de tu divina indiferencia.
Mira las tristes piedras que llevamos
Ya sobre nuestros hombros para enterrar tus dones:
La hermosura, la verdad, la justicia, cuyo afán imposible
Tú sólo eras capaz de infundir en nosotros.
Si ellas murieran hoy, de la memoria tú te borrarías
Como un sueño remoto de los hombres que fueron.

The Clouds

But how can we appease you, God?
You were my thirst, my lost love,
My broken house, my weary life, and the house and life
Of many men adrift like me
With the shipwreck of this nation. Arrayed
Like playing cards, my meager paradises fell
One by one. Was it your hand that stirred the air,
Toppling them? In the deep void, the abysmal
      depression,
Beyond them all, does the cloud that hides you
Rise at last, before me?

Do not strike me down in anger.
Who will be love in your world, if not you?
Pity us for once, listen to the murmur
That rises like a wave
And rolls to the foot of your divine indifference.
Behold these sad stones we bear on our backs
Already, to bury the gifts you have given us.
Beauty, justice, truth — only you
Could instill in us their impossible travail.
If they were to die today, you would be blotted out
From memory, a dim dream of dead men.

CORDURA

Suena la lluvia oscura.
El campo amortecido
Inclina hacia el invierno
Cimas densas de árboles.

Los cristales son bruma
Donde un iris mojado
Refleja ramas grises,
Humo de hogares, nubes.

A veces, por los claros
Del cielo, la amarilla
Luz de un edén perdido
Aún baja a las praderas.

Un hondo sentimiento
De alegrías pasadas,
Hechas olvido bajo
Tierra, llena la tarde.

Turbando el aire quieto
Con una queja ronca,
Como sombras, los cuervos
Agudos, giran, pasan.

Voces tranquilas hay
De hombres, hacia lo lejos,
Que el suelo están labrando
Como hicieron los padres.

COMMON SENSE

The dark rain drums.
The attenuated fields
Tip their thick treetops
Toward winter.

The window panes are a mist
Where a wet luster
Reflects gray branches,
Chimney-smoke, clouds.

At times, the yellow
Light of a lost Eden
Still descends to the plains
Through clearing skies.

The afternoon brims
With a powerful sense
Of past happiness, now changed
To oblivion under the earth.

Breaking the still air
With a raucous cry,
The clever crows
Wheel and pass like shadows.

From the distance
Come quiet voices of men
Tilling the earth
As their fathers did.

Sus manos, si se extienden,
Hallan manos amigas.
Su fe es la misma. Juntos
viven la misma espera.

Allá, sobre la lluvia,
Donde anidan estrellas,
Dios por su cielo mira
Dulces rincones grises.

Todo ha sido creado,
Como yo, de la sombra;
Esta tierra a mí ajena,
Estos cuerpos ajenos.

Un sueño, que conmigo
Él puso para siempre,
Me aísla. Así está el chopo
Entre encinas robustas.

Duro es hallarse solo
En medio de los cuerpos.
Pero esa forma tiene
Su amor: la cruz sin nadie.

Por ese amor espero,
Despierto en su regazo,
Hallar un alba pura
Comunión con los hombres.

Mas la luz deja el campo.
Es tarde y nace el frío.
Cerrada está la puerta,
Alumbrando la lámpara.

Por las sendas sombrías
Se duele el viento ahora
Como alma aislada en lucha.
La noche será breve.

The Clouds

If they reach out,
They find friendly hands.
Their faith is unchanged.
Together they live the same expectancy.

There, where the stars nest
Above the rain,
God gazes from heaven
At mild gray corners.

Like me, everything
Has come from shadow:
This earth alien to me,
These alien bodies.

A dream
He put in me forever
Isolates me. Like a poplar
Among hearty oaks.

This is hard – to find one's self
Alone amidst other bodies.
But such a love
Has its form: the empty cross.

Through that love,
And awake in its embrace, I hope
To find communion with men
On one pure dawn.

But light leaves the fields.
It is late, the cold is born.
The door is shut,
The lamp flaming up.

Along the dark roads
The wind is tormented now
Like one soul isolated in struggle.
The night will be short.

LÁZARO

Era de madrugada.
Después de retirada la piedra con trabajo,
Porque no la materia sino el tiempo
Pesaba sobre ella,
Oyeron una voz tranquila
Llamándome, como un amigo llama
Cuando atrás queda alguno
Fatigado de la jornada y cae la sombra.
Hubo un silencio largo.
Así lo cuentan ellos que lo vieron.

Yo no recuerdo sino el frío
Extraño que brotaba
Desde la tierra honda, con angustia
De entresueño, y lento iba
A despertar el pecho,
Donde insistió con unos golpes leves,
Ávido de tornarse sangre tibia.
En mi cuerpo dolía
Un dolor vivo o un dolor soñado.

LAZARUS

It was not yet daybreak.
After they labored to withdraw the rock —
For time, not matter,
Weighed it down —
They heard a calm, steady voice
Call me, as when darkness comes
And a friend calls back to one fallen behind,
Worn out by the day's journey.
There was a long silence.
Thus they tell it, who were there.

I remember only the strange
Cold that broke
From the deep earth and with the anguish
Of half-wakening slowly
Began to rouse my breast,
Beating insistently, eager
To turn to warm blood.
A living pain, or a dreamt one,
Wracked my body.

Era otra vez la vida.
Cuando abrí los ojos
Fue el alba pálida quien dijo
La verdad. Porque aquellos
Rostros ávidos, sobre mí estaban mudos,
Mordiendo un sueño vago inferior al milagro,
Como rebaño hosco
Que no a la voz sino a la piedra atiende,
Y el sudor de sus frentes
Oí caer pesado entre la hierba.

Alguien dijo palabras
De nuevo nacimiento.
Mas no hubo allí sangre materna
Ni vientre fecundado
Que crea con dolor nueva vida doliente.
Sólo anchas vendas, lienzos amarillos
Con olor denso, desnudaban
La carne gris y fláccida como fruto pasado;
No el terso cuerpo oscuro, rosa de los deseos,
Sino el cuerpo de un hijo de la muerte.

El cielo rojo abría hacia lo lejos
Tras de olivos y alcores;
El aire estaba en calma.
Mas temblaban los cuerpos,
Como las ramas cuando el viento sopla,
Brotando de la noche con los brazos tendidos
Para ofrecerme su propio afán estéril.
La luz me remordía
Y hundí la frente sobre el polvo
Al sentir la pereza de la muerte.

It was life, one more time.
When I opened my eyes
It was the pale dawn that spoke
That truth — for those
Anxious faces over me were silent
As they gnawed on an uncertain dream somehow less
    than a miracle,
Like a willful flock
That ignores all voices, but will heed a hurled stone;
And I heard the sweat from their foreheads
Fall heavily into the weeds.

Someone said something
About a new birth.
But there was no maternal blood,
No sweet womb
To create, with pain, a new painful life;
Only wide bandages, yellowed cotton
With a thick scent, that left
The soft gray flesh naked, like old fruit.
No smooth dark body, rose of desires,
But the body of a child of death.

In the distance, red sky was breaking
Behind the hills and olive trees.
The air was still.
But their bodies shook
Like branches in the wind
And surged from the night with arms outstretched
To offer me their own sterile solicitude.
The light brought biting remorse
And I laid my forehead in the dust
And felt death's slothfulness.

Quise cerrar los ojos,
Buscar la vasta sombra,
La tiniebla primaria
Que su venero esconde bajo el mundo
Lavando de vergüenzas la memoria.
Cuando un alma doliente en mis entrañas
Gritó, por las oscuras galerías
Del cuerpo, agria, desencajada,
Hasta chocar contra el muro de los huesos
Y levantar mareas febriles por la sangre.

Aquel que con su mano sostenía
La lámpara testigo del milagro,
Mató brusco la llama,
Porque ya el día estaba con nosotros.
Una rápida sombra sobrevino.
Entonces, hondos bajo una frente, vi unos ojos
Llenos de compasión, y hallé temblando un alma
Donde mi alma se copiaba inmensa,
Por el amor dueña del mundo.

Vi unos pies que marcaban la linde de la vida,
El borde de una túnica incolora
Plegada, resbalando
Hasta rozar la fosa, como un ala
Cuando a subir tras de la luz incita.
Sentí de nuevo el sueño, la locura
Y el error de estar vivo,
Siendo carne doliente día a día.
Pero él me había llamado
Y en mí no estaba ya sino seguirle.

The Clouds

I tried to close my eyes,
To find that vast shadow
Primal darkness
That hides its headwaters under the earth
Cleansing memory of shame.
When a tormented soul within me
Cried out through the dark corridors
Of my body — bitter and ghastly
Until it struck the wall of my bones
And moved my blood in febrile tides.

The one who held the lamp —
Witness to the miracle —
Abruptly quenched the flame,
For day had come.
Suddenly there was a shadow.
I saw the compassionate eyes beneath the brow,
And trembling I confronted
A soul in which my own was immensely mirrored
By love, the mistress of the earth.

I saw two feet that marked the frontier of life,
And the hem of a colorless pleated
Tunic, slipping down
To brush the edge of the tomb, like a wing
When it urges a rising into the light.
Then, again, I sensed the dream, the insanity
And mistake of being alive,
Of being tormented flesh day after day.
But he had called me
And I could do nothing but follow.

Por eso, puesto en pie, anduve silencioso,
Aunque todo para mí fuera extraño y vano,
Mientras pensaba: así debieron ellos,
Muerto yo, caminar llevándome a la tierra.
La casa estaba lejos;
Otra vez vi sus muros blancos
Y el ciprés del huerto.
Sobre el terrado había una estrella pálida.
Dentro no hallamos lumbre
En el hogar cubierto de ceniza.

Todos le rodearon en la mesa.
Encontré el pan amargo, sin sabor las frutas,
El agua sin frescor, los cuerpos sin deseo;
La palabra hermandad sonaba falsa,
Y de la imagen del amor quedaban
Sólo recuerdos vagos bajo el viento.
Él conocía que todo estaba muerto
En mí, que yo era un muerto
Andando entre los muertos.

Sentado a su derecha me veía
Como aquel que festejan al retorno.
La mano suya descansaba cerca
Y recliné la frente sobre ella
Con asco de mi cuerpo y de mi alma.
Así pedí en silencio, como se pide
A Dios, porque su nombre,
Más vasto que los templos, los mares, las estrellas,
Cabe en el desconsuelo del hombre que está solo,
Fuerza para llevar la vida nuevamente.

The Clouds

So that, standing up, I walked silently,
Even though, for me, all was strange and empty.
And I thought: so must they have walked
When they carried me, dead, to the grave.
The house was far away;
I saw the white walls again
And the cypress in the garden.
Above the roof a pale star;
Inside, no fire,
The hearth covered with ashes.

Everyone sat around him at the table.
To me the bread was bitter, the fruit tasteless,
The water stale, the bodies without desire;
The word "brotherhood" sounded empty
And of the image of love nothing remained
But vague memories beneath the wind.
He understood that everything was dead
In me, that I was a dead man
Wandering among the dead.

I sat on his right, and I seemed
The prodigal returned, whom everyone entertains.
His hand rested near me
And I laid my forehead on it
Disgusted with my body and my soul.
Thus I silently asked — as one asks
God, for his very name
Is greater than temples, or seas, or stars,
And yet can dwell in the dejection of the lonely —
For the strength to bear life again.

Así rogué, con lágrimas,
Fuerza de soportar mi ignorancia resignado,
Trabajando, no por mi vida ni mi espíritu,
Mas por una verdad en aquellos ojos entrevista
Ahora. La hermosura es paciencia.
Sé que el lirio del campo,
Tras de su humilde oscuridad en tantas noches
Con larga espera bajo tierra,
Del tallo verde erguido a la corola alba
Irrumpe un día en gloria triunfante.

The Clouds

Weeping I pleaded
For the strength to bear my unknowing with resignation,
To work — not for my own life or my spirit —
But for some truth glimpsed in those eyes
At that moment. Beauty is patience.
I know that the lily of the field
After its humble obscurity
Of waiting beneath the earth so many nights,
With green stem rising to the dawn-white blossom
Breaks forth one day in triumphant glory.

IMPRESIÓN DE DESTIERRO

Fue la pasada primavera,
Hace ahora casi un año,
En un salón del viejo Temple, en Londres,
Con viejos muebles. Las ventanas daban,
Tras edificios viejos, a lo lejos,
Entre la hierba el gris relámpago del río.
Todo era gris y estaba fatigado
Igual que el iris de una perla enferma.

Eran señores viejos, viejas damas,
En los sombreros plumas polvorientas;
Un susurro de voces allá por los rincones,
Junto a mesas con tulipanes amarillos,
Retratos de familia y teteras vacías.
La sombra que caía
Con un olor a gato,
Despertaba ruidos en cocinas.

Un hombre silencioso estaba
Cerca de mí. Veía
La sombra de su largo perfil algunas veces
Asomarse abstraído al borde de la taza,
Con la misma fatiga
Del muerto que volviera
Desde la tumba a una fiesta mundana.

IMPRESSION OF EXILE

It was last spring in London,
Almost a year ago now,
At the Inner Temple
In a room of well-worn furniture.
Through the windows and beyond old buildings
One saw grass and the gray flash of the river
In the distance. Everything
Was gray and exhausted
Like the luster of a sick pearl.

They were old gentlemen, old ladies
With dusty feathers in their hats;
Voices murmured in the corners
Next to tables with yellow tulips,
Family portraits and empty teapots.
The shadow that fell
With the smell of a cat
Roused noises in kitchens.

Near me was a taciturn man.
I saw the narrow shadow
Of his profile occasionally rise
Self-engrossed over his teacup
With the fatigue
Of a dead man returned
From the tomb for a worldly celebration.

En los labios de alguno,
Allá por los rincones
Donde los viejos juntos susurraban,
Densa como una lágrima cayendo,
Brotó de pronto una palabra: España.
Un cansancio sin nombre
Rodaba en mi cabeza.
Encendieron las luces. Nos marchamos.

Tras largas escaleras casi a oscuras
Me hallé luego en la calle,
Y a mi lado, al volverme,
Vi otra vez a aquel hombre silencioso,
Que habló indistinto algo
Con acento extranjero,
Un acento de niño en voz envejecida.

Andando me seguía
Como si fuera bajo un peso invisible,
Arrastrando la losa de su tumba;
Mas luego se detuvo.
"¿España?", dijo. "Un nombre.
España ha muerto." Había
Una súbita esquina en la calleja.
Le vi borrarse entre la sombra húmeda.

The Clouds

Over in the corner
Where the old ones buzzed
One word burst from someone's lips
Like a tear distilled from sorrow: Spain.
A weariness without name
Spun in my head.
The lights came on. We left.

Down long half-dark stairs,
Then I found myself in the street,
And as I turned I saw
The silent man at my side again.
He mumbled something
In a foreign accent,
A child's accent in an aged voice.

He followed me
As if alone under an invisible weight,
Dragging the lid of his tomb.
Then he stopped.
"Spain?" he said. "A name.
Spain is dead." There was
A sudden turn in the alley.
I watched him disappear in the damp shadows.

DESEO

Por el campo tranquilo de septiembre,
Del álamo amarillo alguna hoja,
Como una estrella rota,
Girando al suelo viene.

Si así el alma inconsciente,
Señor de las estrellas y las hojas,
Fuese, encendida sombra,
De la vida a la muerte.

DESIRE

In the quiet September countryside
One leaf of the yellow poplar
Comes down
        like a shattered star
Spinning to the ground.

If only the unconscious soul
Lord of leaves and stars
Were thus
        shadow set afire
From life to death.

AMOR OCULTO

Como el tumulto gris del mar levanta
Un alto arco de espuma, maravilla
Multiforme del agua, y ya en la orilla
Roto, otra nueva espuma se adelanta;

Como el campo despierta en primavera
Eternamente, fiel bajo el sombrío
Celaje de las nubes, y al sol frío
Con asfodelos cubre la pradera;

Como el genio en distintos cuerpos nace,
Formas que han de nutrir la antigua gloria
De su fuego, mientras la humana escoria
Sueña ardiendo en la llama y se deshace,

Así siempre, como agua, flor o llama,
Vuelves entre la sombra, fuerza oculta
Del otro amor. El mundo bajo insulta.
Pero la vida es tuya: surge y ama.

CLANDESTINE LOVE

As the sea's gray tumult lifts
A high arch of spume, the water's
Faceted loveliness, that now breaks
On the shore, as another advances;

As the earth always wakes in spring
Steadfast beneath the shadowy
Cloudscape, and in cold sunlight
Covers the plain with asphodels;

As genius is born in different bodies, forms
That will nourish its ancient, fiery glory,
While the merely human dross
Sleeps and is burnt in the flame;

So you always return in shadow
As water, flower, flame, clandestine
Force of an other love. The dull world offends.
But life is yours: come forth and love.

GAVIOTAS EN LOS PARQUES

Dueña de los talleres, las fábricas, los bares,
Toda piedras oscuras bajo un cielo sombrío,
Silenciosa a la noche, los domingos devota,
Es la ciudad levítica que niega sus pecados.

El verde turbio de la hierba y los árboles
Interrumpe con parques los edificios uniformes,
Y en la naturaleza sin encanto, entre la lluvia,
Mira de pronto, penacho de locura, las gaviotas.

¿Por qué, teniendo alas, son huéspedes del humo,
El sucio arroyo, los puentes de madera de estos parques?
Un viento de infortunio o una mano inconsciente,
De los puertos nativos, tierra adentro las trajo.

Lejos quedó su nido de los mares, mecido por tormentas
De invierno, en calma luminosa los veranos.
Ahora su queja va, como el grito de almas en destierro.
Quien con alas las hizo, el espacio les niega.

114

GULLS IN THE PARKS

Mistress of workshops, factories and bars
Lying stone-dark beneath a gloomy sky,
Soundless at night, devout on day-bright sabbath,
The city of Pharisees denies its sins.

Through the buildings' uniform facades
Breaks the ragged green of grass and trees;
Above this charmless scene of lawns and rain
An unexpected, mad panache: the gulls.

Why, having wings, are they the guests of smoke,
The foul streams in the parks, and wooden bridges?
Treacherous winds or some unconscious hand
Cast them inland, far from their native havens.

And the sea-nest is faraway, now rocked
By icy storms or luminous summer peace.
Their cries resound like those of exiled souls.
Whoever gave them wings denies them space.

UN ESPAÑOL HABLA DE SU TIERRA

Las playas, parameras
Al rubio sol durmiendo,
Los oteros, las vegas
En paz, a solas, lejos;

Los castillos, ermitas,
Cortijos y conventos,
La vida con la historia,
Tan dulces al recuerdo,

Ellos, los vencedores
Caínes sempiternos,
De todo me arrancaron.
Me dejan el destierro.

Una mano divina
Tu tierra alzó en mi cuerpo
Y allí la voz dispuso
Que hablase tu silencio.

Contigo solo estaba,
En ti sola creyendo;
Pensar tu nombre ahora
Envenena mis sueños.

Amargos son los días
De la vida, viviendo
Sólo una larga espera
A fuerza de recuerdos.

A SPANIARD SPEAKS OF HIS LAND

Beaches, fastnesses
Asleep in the fair sun,
The hills, the empty,
Distant, peaceful plain;

The castles, hermitages,
Manses and convents,
A life with history,
So pleasing to memory —

But the eternal
Conquering Cains
Have taken everything
From me, and left me exile.

A divine hand
Raised your lands in my body
And there set a voice
That would speak your silence.

I was alone with you,
Believing in you alone;
Now to think your name
Poisons my dreams.

The days of life are bitter,
And living merely
A long expectancy
By dint of memories.

117

Un día, tú ya libre
De la mentira de ellos,
Me buscarás. Entonces
¿Qué ha de decir un muerto?

The Clouds

One day, when you are freed
At last from their lie,
You will seek me out, and then
What will a dead man say?

VIOLETAS

Leves, mojadas, melodiosas,
Su oscura luz morada insinuándose
Tal perla vegetal tras verdes valvas,
Son un grito de marzo, un sortilegio
De alas nacientes por el aire tibio.

Frágiles, fieles, sonríen quedamente
Con muda incitación, como sonrisa
Que brota desde un fresco labio humano.
Mas su forma graciosa nunca engaña:
Nada prometen que después traicionen.

Al marchar victoriosas a la muerte
Sostienen un momento, ellas tan frágiles,
El tiempo entre sus pétalos. Así su instante alcanza,
Norma para lo efímero que es bello,
A ser vivo embeleso en la memoria.

VIOLETS

Frail, glistening, melodious,
Their dark purple light radiating
Like vegetal pearl through green pods,
They are a cry of March, a conjuring
Of incipient wings in the warm air.

Fragile, steadfast, they rejoice gently
With mute urging, like a smile
That brims on cool, human lips.
But their lovely form does not deceive:
They promise nothing they might themselves betray.

As they march victoriously to death,
For a moment, utterly fragile, they sustain
Time among their petals. Thus their instant,
The exemplar of ephemeral beauty, becomes
Ecstatic rapture, alive in memory.

LAS RUINAS

Silencio y soledad nutren la hierba
Creciendo oscura y fuerte entre ruinas,
Mientras la golondrina con grito enajenado
Va por el aire vasto, y bajo el viento
Las hojas en las ramas tiemblan vagas
Como al roce de cuerpos invisibles.

Puro, de plata nebulosa, ya levanta
El agudo creciente de la luna
Vertiendo por el campo paz amiga,
Y en esta luz incierta las ruinas de mármol
Son construcciones bellas, musicales,
Que el sueño completó.

　　　　　　　　　Esto es el hombre. Mira
La avenida de tumbas y cipreses, y las calles
Llevando al corazón de la gran plaza
Abierta a un horizonte de colinas:
Todo está igual, aunque una sombra sea
De lo que fue hace siglos, mas sin gente.

Levanta ese titánico acueducto
Arcos rotos y secos por el valle agreste
Adonde el mirto crece con la anémona,
En tanto el agua libre entre los juncos
Pasa con la enigmática elocuencia
De su hermosura que venció a la muerte.

RUINS

Silence and solitude sustain the grass
That grows among ruins, dark and strong,
While with agitated cries a swallow soars
Through infinite air, and beneath the wind
Leaves tremble dimly on the branches
As if bodies now invisible had touched them.

Of cloudy silver, the pure sharp crescent moon
Rises spilling friendly peace
On the countryside,
And in this uncertain light the marble ruins
Are musical and lovely formations
Brought to completion by a dream.

                    This is what man is. Look,
The avenue of cypresses and tombs,
The streets that lead to the heart of the great square
Open to the bulking hills:
Though a mere shadow of what it was
Centuries ago, it is unchanged. But unpeopled.

The aqueduct of titans, its arches dry
And broken, stands across the rough valley
Where myrtles grow among anemones,
And water freely slips among the reeds
With the enigmatic eloquence
Of a beauty that conquered death.

En las tumbas vacías, las urnas sin cenizas,
Conmemoran aún relieves delicados
Muertos que ya no son sino la inmensa muerte anónima,
Aunque sus prendas leves sobrevivan:
Pomos ya sin perfume, sortijas y joyeles
O el talismán irónico de un sexo poderoso,
Que el trágico desdén del tiempo perdonara.

Las piedras que los pies vivos rozaron
En centurias atrás, aún permanecen
Quietas en su lugar, y las columnas
En la plaza, testigos de las luchas políticas,
Y los altares donde sacrificaron y esperaron,
Y los muros que el placer de los cuerpos recataban.

Tan sólo ellos no están. Este silencio
Parece que aguarda la vuelta de sus vidas.
Mas los hombres, hechos de esa materia fragmentaria
Con que se nutre el tiempo, aunque sean
Aptos para crear lo que resiste al tiempo,
Ellos en cuya mente lo eterno se concibe,
Como en el fruto el hueso encierran muerte.

Oh Dios. Tú que nos has hecho
Para morir, ¿por qué nos infundiste
La sed de eternidad, que hace al poeta?
¿Puedes dejar así, siglo tras siglo,
Caer como vilanos que deshace un soplo
Los hijos de la luz en la tiniebla avara?

On empty tombs, on empty urns,
The delicate reliefs commemorate the dead,
Now no more than one immense
Anonymous death, though their tokens survive:
Trinkets, jewels, empty perfume flasks,
Or the ironic talisman of sexual prowess —
All of which the tragic scorn
Of time has long forgiven.

Stones trodden ages ago
By living feet lie quietly in place,
And colonnades, witnesses of politics and struggle;
And altars where they sacrificed, and waited;
And walls that discreetly hid the pleasures of the body.

Only *they* are missing. This silence
Seems to await the return of life.
But men are made of the splintered stuff
That time feeds on, and though they may
Create that which withstands all time,
Those in whose minds the eternal is conceived
Hide death within, like the pit of a fruit.

O God, you who made us
For dying, why have you put this thirst
For eternity in us, that makes us poets?
Can you allow these sons of light
For centuries and centuries
To fall like thistledown from the stem
Into this greedy darkness?

Mas tú no existes. Eres tan sólo el nombre
Que da el hombre a su miedo y su impotencia,
Y la vida sin ti es esto que parecen
Estas mismas ruinas bellas en su abandono:
Delirio de la luz ya sereno a la noche,
Delirio acaso hermoso cuando es corto y es leve.

Todo lo que es hermoso tiene su instante, y pasa.
Importa como eterno gozar de nuestro instante.
Yo no te envidio, Dios; déjame a solas
Con mis obras humanas que no duran:
El afán de llenar lo que es efímero
De eternidad, vale tu omnipotencia.

Esto es el hombre. Aprende pues, y cesa
De perseguir eternos dioses sordos
Que tu plegaria nutre y tu olvido aniquila.
Tu vida, lo mismo que la flor, ¿es menos bella acaso
Porque crezca y se abra en brazos de la muerte?

Sagrada y misteriosa cae la noche,
Dulce como una mano amiga que acaricia,
Y en su pecho, donde tal ahora yo, otros un día
Descansaron la frente, me reclino
A contemplar sereno el campo y las ruinas.

But you don't exist. You are only the name
Man gives to his own fear and impotence,
And life without you is what these ruins seem
In their beautiful abandonment:
A rapture of the calm nocturnal light,
Perhaps most lovely when it is fleeting.

What is beautiful lives for an instant, and passes.
We must seize the joy of our instant as eternal.
I do not envy you, God. Leave me alone
With my human works that will not endure:
The longing to fill what is ephemeral
With eternity, is worth your omnipotence.

This is what man is. So man must learn,
And stop this endless pursuit of deaf, eternal gods
Who live on his prayers, but are annihilated
By his forgetting. Is this life
Less lovely because it rises and opens
Like a flower in the arms of death?

Sacred and mysterious the night descends
As sweet as a friend's caressing hand;
And on its breast, where many once rested
Their weary heads as I do now,
I lie down to contemplate
In peace the ruins in the fields.

TIERRA NATIVA

A Paquita G. de la Bárcena

Es la luz misma, la que abrió mis ojos
Toda ligera y tibia como un sueño,
Sosegada en colores delicados
Sobre las formas puras de las cosas.

El encanto de aquella tierra llana,
Extendida como una mano abierta,
Adonde el limonero encima de la fuente
Suspendía su fruto entre el ramaje.

El muro viejo en cuya barda abría
A la tarde su flor azul la enredadera,
Y al cual la golondrina en el verano
Tornaba siempre hacia su antiguo nido.

El susurro del agua alimentando,
Con su música insomne en el silencio,
Los sueños que la vida aún no corrompe,
El futuro que espera como página blanca.

Todo vuelve otra vez vivo a la mente,
Irreparable ya con el andar del tiempo,
Y su recuerdo ahora me traspasa
El pecho tal puñal fino y seguro.

Raíz del tronco verde, ¿quién la arranca?
Aquel amor primero, ¿quién lo vence?
Tu sueño y tu recuerdo, ¿quién lo olvida,
Tierra nativa, más mía cuanto más lejana?

NATIVE LAND

To Paquita G. de la Bárcena

It was the light itself that opened
My eyes, airy and cool as a dream,
In delicate colors at rest
Upon the pure forms of things.

The spell of those wide, rolling plains,
Spread out like an open hand,
Where over the spring the lemon tree's
Pendulous fruit hung in the foliage.

The old wall in whose thatch at dusk
The blue vine flower bloomed,
And where the swallow returned
Each summer to last year's nest.

And in the midst of silence, where water purled,
Unsleeping music nourishing the dreams
Not yet tainted by life, the future
That waited like an empty page.

Alive, it all returns to the mind,
Unattainable now time has passed;
Like a sharp sure dagger
Its memory pierces my breast.

Root of the green tree trunk — who tears it out?
That first love — who overcomes it now?
Your dream and memory — who can forget them,
My native land? — the more mine as more distant.

JARDÍN

Desde un rincón sentado,
Mira la luz, la hierba,
Los troncos, la musgosa
Piedra que mide el tiempo

Al sol en la glorieta,
Y las ninfeas, copos
De sueño sobre el agua
Inmóvil de la fuente.

Allá en lo alto la trama
Traslúcida de hojas,
El cielo con su pálido
Azul, las nubes blancas.

Un mirlo dulcemente
Canta, tal la voz misma
Del jardín que te hablara.
En la hora apacible

Mira bien con tus ojos,
Como si acariciaras
Todo. Gratitud debes
De tan puro sosiego,

Libre de gozo y pena,
A la luz, porque pronto
Tal tú de aquí, se parte.
A lo lejos escuchas

A GARDEN

From the corner where you sit,
Look out at the light,
The grass and trees and mossy
Stone in the arbor

That measures time in the sun,
And the water lilies, tufts
Of dream on the motionless
Water of the fountain.

Above you, the translucent
Folds and pleats of the leaves,
The pale blue of the sky,
White clouds.

A blackbird sweetly
Sings, as if the voice
Of the garden were to speak to you.
In such a still hour

Use your eyes well, look
As if you gently touched
Each thing. You owe thanks —
For such pure calm

Free from pleasure or pain —
To the light, for soon
It will go, as you will.
In the distance you hear

La pisada ilusoria
Del tiempo, que se mueve
Hacia el invierno. Entonces
Tu pensamiento y este

Jardín que así contemplas
Por la luz traspasado,
Han de yacer con largo
Sueño, mudos, sombríos.

As One Awaiting Dawn

The deceptive tread
Of time, moving
Toward winter. Then
Both your meditation and this

Garden you contemplate,
Transfixed by the light,
Must lie down in a long
Sleep, mute and dark.

TARDE OSCURA

Lo mismo que un sueño
Al cuerpo separa
Del alma, esta niebla
Tierra y luz aparta.

Todo es raro y vago;
Ni són en el viento,
Latido en el agua,
Color en el suelo.

De sí mismo extraño,
¿Sabes lo que espera
El pájaro quieto
Por la rama seca?

Lejos, tras un vidrio,
Una luz ya arde,
Poniendo la hora
Más incierta. Yace

La vida, y tú solo,
No muerto, no vivo,
En el pecho sientes
Débil su latido.

Por estos suburbios
Sórdidos, sin norte
Vas, como el destino
Inútil del hombre.

DUSK

The way dream
Parts body from soul,
This mist
Separates earth and light.

Everything is blurred and strange;
The silent breeze,
Motionless water
And earth void of color.

Do you know
What that quiet bird
Awaits on its dry twig,
Estranged from itself?

Afar, behind a window
A burning lamp
Makes the hour uncertain.
Life lies

Down, and alone,
Neither living nor dead,
You feel its weak beating
In your body.

You roam these sordid
Outskirts aimlessly,
Like the directionless fate
Of man himself.

Y en el pensamiento
Luz o fe ahora
Buscas, mientras vence
Afuera la sombra.

As One Awaiting Dawn

In your mind, you search
For light or faith,
While outside
Darkness slowly conquers.

APOLOGIA PRO VITA SUA

Abrid las puertas, dejad que vuelvan todos;
Su número es bien corto. Como en otro tiempo,
Espacio suficiente habría para ellos
Adentro de mi amor; después ninguno ha entrado
Allá durante años. Igual es a una casa
Que el dueño olvida, ausente en otras tierras,
Donde nada interrumpe el gobernar oscuro
Del ratón, la polilla y telarañas,
Sino el rayo de sol, cuando penetra
Furtivo en el desván por un postigo hendido
Para agitar los sueños del polvo en formas grises;
O la rama de espino florido en primavera,
Contagiada del viento su locura,
Llamando persistente a los cristales, ciegos
Ante el albor perlado o la luna amarilla.

Dejadles que se acerquen a mi cama
Y alumbren sus semblantes, como estrellas
Suspensas en la noche sobre el agua oscura,
La agonía de aquel que les amara,
Uniéndoles así, desconocidos los unos a los otros,
En apretados haces de recuerdos.
Primero vienes tú, dame la mano, Arcángel,
Porque ya no conozco si te amaba o te odiaba,
Y perdón es ahora lo único que importa,
Antes de que a mi alma la destrone el olvido,
Cuyos pasos se acercan, rotos al fin muros y centinelas.
Si el amor no es un hombre, una experiencia inútil de
        los labios
(Así los dedos clavan un ala trasparente
Tras el cristal curioso de algún laboratorio),
Yo creo que te he amado. Mas eso ya no importa.

APOLOGIA PRO VITA SUA

Open the doors! Let them all come back in;
They are precious few. Just as before,
There would be room enough for them
In my love; no one has gone in there
For years. It is like a house
The landlord, living somewhere else, forgets.
Nothing interrupts the dark governing
Of rat, moth, and cobweb
But the sun, when its rays furtively pierce
A warped shutter, penetrate the garret,
And stir up the dreams of the dust in gray shapes.
Or the branch of flowering hawthorn in spring
Insistently tapping the glass
With a madness caught from the wind.
And the windowpanes are blind
To the pearly dawn and yellow moon.

Let them come near my bed,
And throw the light on their faces!
Like stars hanging over dark water . . .
They are united now by the agony
Of him who loved them, though they be unknown
To each other, a close-tied sheaf of memories.
First you, give me your hand, Archangel,
I cannot recall whether I loved or hated you,
And now all that's important is pardon,
Before oblivion overthrows my soul.
I hear it coming closer, past defeated walls
And sentinels. If love is not a man,
A futile sensation of the lips
(Thus fingers clasp a transparent wing
Behind the curious glass of some laboratory)
Then I believe I have loved you. No matter, now.

Deja pasar aquellos que ocuparon
Luego tu ausencia. Así al morir un rey
Otro ciñó la espada y la corona,
Sonando hacia la luna trompas en regocijo,
Aunque fuera excesivo para el nuevo monarca
El destino primero de aquel héroe,
Quien a sí mismo alzándose, alzó a sus sucesores
En el nombre, ya que no en la pasión dominadora.
¿No es la pasión medida de la grandeza humana
Y acero templado por su fuego el alma grande?
A mí esos otros cuerpos me enseñaron
Que si amor palidece, cuando ya es imposible
Creer en la verdad de quien se ama,
Crece aún el deseo, y vence con un fuego
Presagio de aquéllos en infierno ya sin esperanza.

Detrás venís vosotros, los amigos.
Qué dicen esos ojos aún claro lo recuerdo:
Si afuera es violento el mediodía,
Entra aquí. Facilidad sedante te brindamos;
Bodas de sombra y luz engendran la penumbra
Propicia a confidencias perezosas,
Y al nuevo visitante todo espera:
Asiento muelle, la copa con el vino,
Allá al rincón dormidas lilas blancas.
Benevolencia tibia le sienta bien al cuerpo
Que por desierto al sol ha caminado solo.
Después del purgatorio ¿no ha de ser grato el limbo?
Mas respeta la seña de esta hermandad, la tuya
Si a la pasión renuncias. Y nuestro olvido
Ha de vencer un día a tu memoria.

Let those who later took your place
Come near. When one king died
Did not another buckle on the sword and don the crown,
With trumpets sounding to the moon in jubilation? —
Even though the destiny of that first hero
Were too great for any new monarch. The first
Had raised himself up, and raised his successors
In name, if not in the reigning passion.
Is not passion the measure of human greatness?
And in its fire, the great soul tempered steel?
Those other bodies taught me
That if love pales, when it is impossible
To believe in the truth of the beloved,
Desire grows greater still, and conquers
With fire the portent of those hopeless many in hell.

Come near, now, friends.
I clearly remember what those eyes say:
If the day is violent outside,
Come in. We'll give you comfort and ease;
The marriage of darkness and light
Engenders the proper shadow
For lazy secrets,
And everything awaits the new caller:
Deep armchair, a glass of wine,
White lilacs asleep in the corner.
Cool benevolence soothes the body
That has traveled alone through sun-struck desert.
After purgatory — will not limbo be bliss?
But honor the sign of this brotherhood — it is yours too
If you renounce passion. And our forgetting
Must defeat your memory someday.

La razón era vuestra, mis amigos:
Es el olvido la verdad más alta.
De todos esos años ya pasados,
Llevándose mi vida, sólo quedan,
Como cirio que arde en cueva oscura
Y mueve sombras vagas sobre el muro,
Recuerdos destinados a morir de mi olvido.
Yo los guardaba, como algunos guardan
Su amor, su ambición otros o su odio;
Valor, ninguno tienen. Y entre ellos,
Sueños brotados de las puertas córneas
Que amarga aquél brotado de puertas marfileñas,
Surgen dolientes esas sombras postreras:
Las sombras de la gente de mi sangre,
Clamando identidad que el alma desconoce.

Caminar a la muerte no es tan fácil,
Y si es duro vivir, morir tampoco es menos.
La llegada a esa meta final pudieron otros
Aliviarla, ya rota la cadena, el eslabón doliente
De la conciencia propia; no asistieron
Como yo insobornables al vencimiento amargo
De la muerte, renunciando a sus almas
Con adiós inconsciente. Yo contemplo
La mía, como pájaro herido bajo un ala
Que a tierra viene, mas lucha todavía
Con plumas abolidas que no sostiene el aire.
Cuán hermosa la luz parece ahora
Temblando en halo azul tras de las ramas
Pardas de invierno donde brilla el hielo.
La renuncia a la luz más que la muerte es dura.

You were right, my friends:
Oblivion is the highest truth.
Of all those past years, carrying with them
My life, there remain —
Like the wavering shadows
Cast on the wall of a cave by a candle —
Only memories destined to die of my forgetting.
I have kept them as others keep
Love, ambition, or hatred;
They are worthless. From among them —
Countless dreams springing from the gates of horn,
But embittered by one dream from the gates of ivory —
These latterly shadows painfully surge:
Shadows of those of my blood,
Clamoring for a recognition the soul denies.

The road to death is not so easy;
If life is difficult, death is not less so.
Others might ease their arrival at that final line,
The chain, the aching last link
Of their own conscience broken; unlike me they did not
Attend, insubordinate, the bitter conquest of death,
Renouncing their souls
With a thoughtless farewell. I contemplate
My own, like a wounded bird with wings
Falling earthward — but still it struggles
With its ruined plumes the air cannot sustain.
How lovely the light seems now
Trembling in blue halos behind the brown
Branches of winter where the ice shines.
To renounce the light is more difficult than dying.

Sólo resta decir: me pesan los pecados
Que la ocasión o fuerza de cometer no tuve.
He vivido sin ti, mi Dios, pues no ayudaste
Esta incredulidad que hizo triste mi alma.
Heme aquí ya vencido, presa fácil ahora
De tus ministros, cuyas manos alzadas
Remiten o condenan a los actos del hombre.
Pero ¿quién es el hombre para juzgar al hombre?
La oración de la fe salva al enfermo,
Y si cayó en pecado le será perdonado.
Este cuerpo que ya sus elementos restituye
Al agua, al aire, al fuego y a la tierra,
Puede la gracia sellarlo todavía con un beso,
Por la virtud de aquel oscuro jugo de la oliva
Ungiendo al luchador y al moribundo.

Bien está que la sangre de la tierra
Moje y perdone al hombre cuando muere,
Aún turbias entreabriendo sus puertas los sentidos,
Y en ellas trace un dedo el signo mágico
Con el óleo más puro: sobre los ojos, que miraron
La luz y la hermosura, codiciándolas;
Sobre el oído, concha de la voz y la música;
Sobre el repliegue de la nariz, abierto
Al aroma del nardo, del cuerpo y de la lluvia;
Sobre la boca, que cantó, que besara y que mintiera;
Sobre la mano, de seda y de metales ambiciosa;
Sobre la espalda, árbol trémulo del espasmo.
Como un vuelo dibuja por el aire,
No la forma del ave, sino el surco efímero,
Desertan los recuerdos en nube mi memoria.

Now there is only this to say: I am oppressed by the sins
I had neither the chance nor the strength to commit.
I have lived without you, my God,
Since you would not help relieve this disbelief
That has made my soul so morose.
Here I am, beaten, an easy victim now
Of your minions, whose raised hands
Acquit or condemn the acts of man.
But who is man to judge man?
Prayer saves the sick
And the sinner is pardoned.
This body that already begins to restore
Elemental water, air, fire and earth to their origins,
Grace could seal still with a touch of its lips,
By virtue of that dark olive oil
Anointing the warrior and the moribund.

It is well that this blood of the earth
Bathes and pardons the dying man,
And with pure oil traces the magic sign
As the senses open their confused doors:
Over the eye which saw
Light and beauty and craved them:
Over the ear, a conch of voice and music;
Over the fluted nose, open
To the scent of spikenard, of the body, of rain;
Over the mouth that sang, or kissed, or lied;
Over the hand, covetous of silk and alloys;
Over the back, the tremulous tree of spasms.
The way flight traces in air
Not the form of the bird but its ephemeral path,
Memories desert my mind in clouds.

Para morir el hombre de Dios no necesita,
Mas Dios para vivir necesita del hombre.
Cuando yo muera, ¿el polvo dirá sus alabanzas?
Quien su verdad declare, ¿será el polvo?
Ida la imagen queda ciego el espejo.
No destruyas mi alma, oh Dios, si es obra de tus manos;
Sálvala con tu amor, donde no prevalezcan
En ella las tinieblas con su astucia profunda,
Y témplala con tu fuego hasta que pueda un día
Embeberse en la luz por ti creada.
Si dijiste, mi Dios, cómo ninguno
De los que en ti confíen ha de ser desolado,
Tras esta noche oscura vendrá el alba
Y hallaremos en ti resurrección y vida.
Para que entre la luz abrid las puertas.

To die, man has no need of God,
But God needs men in order to live.
When I die will dust sing his praises?
And who will speak his truth — the dust?
The mirror is blind once the image is gone.
If my soul is the work of your hands, God, do not
      destroy it;
Save it with your love, where darkness
And darkness' deep craft do not prevail within it,
And temper it with your fire until
It be absorbed utterly in the light you create.
My God, if you have said that no one
Need be desolate who confides in you,
Then after this dark night will come the dawn
And we will find resurrection and life in you.
Open the doors! And let in the light.

EL INDOLENTE

Con hombres como tú el comercio sería
Cosa leve y tan pura que, sin sudor ni sangre
De ninguno comprada, dejaría a la tierra
Intactos sus veneros. Pero a tu pobreza
El comercio podría allanarle un camino.

Durante las tardes meridionales del verano,
A través de una clara ciudad, solas las calles,
Llevarías en cestillo guirnaldas de jazmines,
Y magnolias, por un nido fragante de hojas verdes
Oculto su blancor, como alas de paloma.

Tras de las rejas bajas, si una mujer quisiera
Para su gracia oscura tal vez la fresca gala
De una flor, y prenderla en su pelo o en su pecho,
Donde ha de parecer nieve sobre la tierra,
Una moneda a cambio dejaría en tus manos.

Así, al ponerse la tarde, tú podrías
De un vino trasparente beber el calor rubio,
Mordiendo la delicia de un pan y de una fruta,
Y luego silencioso, tendido junto al río,
Ver latir en la honda noche las estrellas.

THE INDOLENT ONE

With men like you, all commerce would be
A slight, pure thing that, without the purchase
Of anyone's sweat or blood, would leave the earth's
Rich lodes untouched. But commerce could
Make straight a road for your own poverty.

On southern summer afternoons,
Through the transparent city's empty streets
You'd carry a basket filled with garlands
Of jasmine and magnolia, their whiteness concealed
Like a dove's wings in the sweet-smelling green.

Behind the low, wrought-iron gate, a woman —
If she wished the fresh adornment of a flower
For her dark loveliness, to pin in her hair
Or at her breast, where it must seem like snow
On the earth — in trade would leave a coin in your hand.

Later, at dusk, you would be able to drink
Down the gold warmth of a clear wine,
To delight in the taste of bread and fruit,
And then you'd lie in silence by the river
And watch the stars throbbing in the deep night.

AMANDO EN EL TIEMPO

El tiempo, insinuándose en tu cuerpo,
Como nube de polvo en fuente pura,
Aquella gracia antigua desordena
Y clava en mí una pena silenciosa.

Otros antes que yo vieron un día,
Y otros luego verán, cómo decae
La amada forma esbelta, recordando
De cuánta gloria es cifra un cuerpo hermoso.

Pero la vida solos la aprendemos,
Y placer y dolor se ofrecen siempre
Tal mundo virgen para cada hombre;
Así mi pena inculta es nueva ahora.

Nueva como lo fuese al primer hombre,
Que cayó con su amor del paraíso,
Cuando viera, su cielo ya vencido
Por sombras, decaer el cuerpo amado.

TO LOVE IN TIME

Gathering slowly, time clouds your body
Like dust in the pure water of a fountain;
It dishevels an earlier grace
And transfixes me with silent grief.

Before me, others have seen, and others
Will see one day, how the lissome
Beloved form decays, recalling
That a lovely body is the cipher of such glory!

Pleasure and pain are always given
To each of us as virgin realms, as each
Must learn in solitude to live;
Thus now my clumsy grief is new.

As new as when the first man fell
With his love from paradise, as he saw—
His heaven dark with defeat—
The beloved body begin its decay.

EL CEMENTERIO

En torno de la iglesia esparce el cementerio
Sus tumbas viejas, caídas en la hierba
Como lebrel cansado ante los pies del dueño,
Y tras su tapia va la calleja solitaria.

Hay un fulgor aún tras del pino señero
Sobre las losas, adonde los pájaros regresan
Al cobijo nocturno, y un mirlo todavía
Canta. Pero la luz se queda enamorada.

Como un óleo de paz, luz, música y aroma
Traspasan esta hierba, bajo la cual el sueño
De amigos invisibles, que vivieron sus días
Antes que tú, acaso en un recuerdo se despierte.

Ése es todo el paisaje, cuando aquí en la ventana,
Junto al ramo de lilas, mientras la noche viene
Por el aire celeste, mojado y luminoso,
Escuchando al piano dejas ponerse el día.

Piensas entonces cercana la frontera
Donde unida está ya con la muerte la vida,
Y adivinas los cuerpos iguales a simiente,
Que sólo ha de vivir si muere en tierra oscura.

THE CEMETERY

Around the church the cemetery scatters
Its ancient tombs now fallen in the grass
Like exhausted greyhounds at their masters' feet,
And, beyond the wall, the empty alley runs.

The light glows still behind the single pine
Standing above the graves, where birds return
Each night to roost in shelter. There a blackbird
Is singing still. The loving light remains.

The music, light and scent sink in the grass,
A balm of peace. And underneath, the sleep
Of unseen friends who lived before you breaks
Perhaps, disturbed at last by memory.

And all of this is landscape: at the window,
By the lilac branch, you stand and see bright night
Come near through damp celestial air, and now
You listen to the piano, and let day end.

For now the line is near where life with death
Will be united soon, you suddenly think,
Divining that these bodies are like seed
That to be born must die in this dark earth.

EL VIENTO Y EL ALMA

Con tal vehemencia el viento
Viene del mar, que sus sones
Elementales contagian
El silencio de la noche.

Solo en tu cama le escuchas
Insistente en los cristales
Tocar, llorando y llamando
Como perdido sin nadie.

Mas no es él quien en desvelo
Te tiene, sino otra fuerza
De que tu cuerpo es hoy cárcel,
Fue viento libre, y recuerda.

WIND AND SOUL

The wind comes off the sea
With such flapping violence
That its elemental noise spreads
Like disease in the dark silence.

Alone in bed, you listen
As it beats against the windows
Sobbing and calling insistently
As if lost and friendless.

But that's not what it is
Keeps you awake — another
Force confined in your body
Was once unbridled wind, and remembers.

ESCULTURA INACABADA
(David-Apolo, de Miguel Ángel)

Sorprendido, ah sorprendido
Desnudo, en una pausa,
Por la selva remota,
Traspuesto el tiempo.

Adherido a la tierra
Todavía, al tronco
Y a la roca, en la frontera
De infancia a mocedades.

Es el instante, el alba
Pura del cuerpo,
En el secreto absorto
De lo que es virgen.

Reposo y movimiento
Coinciden, ya en los brazos,
El sexo, flor no abierta,
O los muslos, arco de lira.

Por el dintel suspenso
De su propia existencia,
Se mira ensimismado
Y a sí se desconoce.

Dentro, en el pensamiento,
Escucha a su destino,
Caída la cabeza,
Entornados los ojos.

UNFINISHED STATUE
(Michelangelo's *David-Apollo*)

Surprised, ah surprised
Naked, beyond time,
While paused
In remote wilderness.

Still rooted to the earth,
To tree-trunk
And rock, on the frontier
Between childhood and youth.

It is the instant — the pure
Dawn of the body,
The astonished secret —
Of the virgin.

Repose and movement
Coincide, now in arms,
In sex — unopened flower —
Or thighs, the bows of a lyre.

At the lintel of his own existence
He hesitates, wholly self-involved.
He stares at himself
And fails to recognize.

Head fallen,
Eyes half-closed,
Lost in thought he listens
Inwardly to his own fate.

Calla. Que no despierte,
Cuando cae en el tiempo,
Ya sus eternidades
Perdidas hoy.

Mas tú mira, contempla
Largo esa hermosura,
Que la pasión ignora;
Contempla, voz y llanto.

Fue amor quien la trajera,
Amor, la sola fuerza humana,
Desde el no ser, al sueño
Donde latente asoma.

Living Without Being Alive

Hush. Let him not wake
When he falls into time.
Already his eternities
Are lost this very day.

But you must contemplate
At length that beauty
That knows no passion;
Contemplate: voice and lament.

Love, the only human power,
Has brought it here:
From nothingness to this slumber
Where, latent still, yet it emerges.

159

LIMBO

A Octavio Paz

La plaza sola (gris el aire,
Negros los árboles, la tierra
Manchada por la nieve),
Parecía, no realidad, mas copia
Triste sin realidad. Entonces,
Ante el umbral, dijiste:
Viviendo aquí serías
Fantasma de ti mismo.

Inhóspita en su adorno
Parsimonioso, porcelanas, bronces,
Muebles chinos, la casa
Oscura toda era,
Pálidas sus ventanas sobre el río,
Y el color se escondía
En un retablo español, en un lienzo
Francés, su brío amedrentado.

Entre aquellos despojos,
Provecto, el dueño estaba
Sentado junto a su retrato
Por artista a la moda en años idos,
Imagen fatua y fácil
Del *dilettante*, divertido entonces
Comprando lo que una fe creara
En otro tiempo y otra tierra.

LIMBO

To Octavio Paz

The empty plaza — gray air,
Black trees, earth
Stained with snow —
Seemed not reality but a wretched
Unreal copy. Then
At the threshold, you said:
"You'd be a ghost
Of yourself if you lived here."

Uninviting, with its parsimonious
Decorations — porcelains, bronzes,
Chinese furniture — the house
Was completely dark;
The windows over the river were pale,
And in a Spanish *retablo,* a French
Canvas, the color had hidden itself,
Its brio cowering.

In the midst of the cast-off shabbiness
Sat the successful host,
Near his portrait, done by an artist
Out of fashion now,
A fatuous and facile image
Of the dilettante who had merrily
Bought up that which,
In another time, another country,
Had been created out of faith.

Allí con sus iguales,
Damas imperativas bajo sus afeites,
Caballeros seguros de sí mismos,
Rito social cumplía,
Y entre el diálogo moroso,
Tú oyendo alguien que dijo: "Me ofrecieron
La primera edición de un poeta raro,
Y la he comprado," tu emoción callaste.

Así, pensabas, el poeta
Vive para esto, para esto
Noches y días amargos, sin ayuda
De nadie, en la contienda
Adonde, como el fénix, muere y nace,
Para que años después, siglos
Después, obtenga al fin el displicente
Favor de un grande en este mundo.

Su vida ya puede excusarse,
Porque ha muerto del todo;
Su trabajo ahora cuenta,
Domesticado para el mundo de ellos,
Como otro objeto vano,
Otro ornamento inútil;
Y tú cobarde, mudo
Te despediste ahí, como el que asiente,
Más allá de la muerte, a la injusticia.

Mejor la destrucción, el fuego.

Your Hours Are Numbered

There with his equals,
Imperious ladies under their cosmetics,
Self-assured gentlemen,
He sat and fulfilled his social duty,
And in a lethargic dialogue
You heard someone say, "They offered me
The first edition of a rare poet,
And I bought it," and you quelled your feelings.

So, you thought, the poet
Lives for this, for this
The bitter nights and days, with no one's
Help in the fray
Where like a phoenix he dies and is born —
So that, years later, centuries
Later, he may at last obtain the ill-humored
Favor of some earthly grandee.

His life needs no excuse now,
For he is completely dead,
Now it is his work that counts,
Domesticated for their world,
Another vain object,
Another useless ornament.
And cowardly and mute,
Like one who assents
To injustice from beyond death,
You said good-bye.

Better destruction, better fire.

Poemas para un cuerpo: IX

DE DÓNDE VIENES

Si alguna vez te oigo
Hablar de padre, madre, hermanos,
Mi imaginar no vence a la extrañeza
De que sea tu existir originado en otros,
En otros repetido,
Cuando único me parece,
Creado por mi amor; igual al árbol,
A la nube o al agua
Que están ahí, mas nuestros
Son y vienen de nosotros
Porque una vez les vimos
Como jamás les viera nadie antes.

Un puro conocer te dio la vida.

Poems For a Body: IX

WHERE ARE YOU FROM

Whenever I hear you
Speak of father, mother, brothers,
My imagination cannot overcome its surprise
That your being originated in others,
Is repeated in others,
When to me it seems unique,
Created by my love; like the tree,
The cloud, the waters
That are just there, but which are
Ours and come from us
Because we have seen them once
As no one had before.

It was pure knowing that gave you life.

PEREGRINO

¿Volver? Vuelva el que tenga
Tras largos años, tras un largo viaje,
Cansancio del camino y la codicia
De su tierra, su casa, sus amigos,
Del amor que al regreso fiel le espere.

Mas ¿tú? ¿Volver? Regresar no piensas,
Sino seguir libre adelante,
Disponible por siempre, mozo a viejo,
Sin hijo que te busque, como a Ulises,
Sin Ítaca que aguarde y sin Penélope.

Sigue, sigue adelante y no regreses,
Fiel hasta el fin del camino y tu vida,
No eches de menos un destino más fácil,
Tus pies sobre la tierra antes no hollada,
Tus ojos frente a lo antes nunca visto.

PILGRIM

Go back? Let him return
Who, after many years, is tired of the road
And the long journey, and covets
Homeland, house, and friends, the love
That still awaits his faithful reappearance.

But you? Go back? You do not think of returning,
But of going on freely, ever open, ready,
Whether as youth or dotard, with no son
To seek you as Odysseus was sought for,
No waiting Ithaca, no Penelope.

Onward, onward, do not turn back,
Follow this road to the end, this life.
Do not long for any easier fate:
Your feet tread trackless earth,
Your eyes survey what none has ever seen.

TIEMPO DE VIVIR, TIEMPO DE DORMIR

Ya es noche. Vas a la ventana.
El jardín está oscuro abajo.
Ves el lucero de la tarde
Latiendo en fulgor solitario.

Y quietamente te detienes.
Dentro de ti algo se queja:
Esa hermosura no atendida
Te seduce y reclama afuera.

Encanto de estar vivo, el hombre
Sólo siente en raros momentos
Y aún necesita compartirlos
Para aprender la sombra, el sueño.

TIME TO LIVE, TIME TO SLEEP

Now it is night. You go to the window.
The garden lies below in darkness.
You see the evening star begin
To throb in brilliant isolation.

And, silent for a moment, you pause.
Something in you is discontented.
Outside, that unattended beauty
Captivates you, claims you.

Seldom is man aware of life's
Enchantment — yet for him
To learn of shadow and of sleep,
Such moments must be shared.

NOTES TO THE POEMS
AND TRANSLATIONS

The following notes supply the reader with literal renderings of passages that in translation are somewhat at variance with the original text, and with elucidation of some difficulties.

The text from which the Spanish poems are taken is *La realidad y el deseo*. Cernuda issued his collected poems under the title *Reality and Desire* three times during his lifetime, and certain volumes of his work appeared only in these collected poems, as the successive editions were expanded. After his death, the final complete collection was issued, and the present texts and page references are to this last edition (Mexico: Fondo de Cultura Económica, 1970).

VIII

Literally,
> Glass (crystal *or* drop) of water in (a)
>> hand of tedium (*or* boredom, loathing,
>> weariness).
> Already the clouds return in coveys
> Through the sky, with covered (*or* concealed)
>> lights
> Fleeing on the pavement wildly (*or* in
>> delirium).
>
> And the flight inward. The cold surrounds (*or*
>> clenches),
> Slow reptile, its congealed furies.
> Solitude, behind closed doors,
> Throws a light over the empty paper.
>
> The words that veil (*or* stand awake over)
>> the secret

Pleasure, and the virgin lip does not know it;
The dream (*or* sleep), enraptured and
     indolent,

Among its own fogs (*or* mists) goes subject,
Refusing to die. And there only remains
The fleeting beauty beneath the forehead.

This difficult poem presents many of the themes and motifs present in Cernuda's entire *oeuvre:* tedium, clouds, inner withdrawal, solitude, closed doors (like walls), lips, dream, indolence, rapture, fog, death, fleeting beauty.

X

Lines 15-16: literally, "A new love is reborn / To prostrate sense (*or* meaning)." These cryptic lines, somewhat typical of Cernuda in this volume, require a certain amount of ironing-out intranslation, for *resurgir* is not a transitive verb.

The *Al* in line 16 seems to act however to direct the verb's action toward its object. Cernuda more than once uses transitive verbs intransitively (as in "Dejadme solo" in *Un río, un amor* where he writes "una dice, otra dice") and vice versa.

20: *se deja* could mean "allows itself, ceases, abandons itself." The idiomatic English "lets go" seemed best for this word of many meanings.

It should be remarked that VIII and X represent two of the three stanzaic patterns used in *First Poems.* Poems of five stanzas of four lines each of seven syllables (like X) alternate with *décimas,* poems of ten lines each of eight syllables. The longer poems are in assonance in even-numbered lines; the *décimas* rhyme ABBAACC DDC. The third form is the sonnet, of which there are two, the eighth and nineteenth poems of the sequence, which do not interrupt the alternation of the other two forms in the sequence. It is a volume that is extremely consistent in its themes and poetic recourses.

Remorse in Black Tie

This ambiguous poem is best served by a literal rendering here:

> A gray man advances through the street of mist
>   (*or* fog);
> No-one suspects it (*or* him). He is an
>   empty body;
> Empty as plains, as sea, as wind,
> Such harsh deserts beneath an implacable sky.
>
> It is (*or* he is) past time, and now his
>   wings
> Among shadow (s) find a pale force;
> It is remorse, which by night, doubting,
> In secret brings near its
>   careless (*or* thoughtless,
>   unsuspecting, etc.) shadow.
>
> Do not take that hand. The ivy haughtily
> Will rise covering the trunks of winter.
> Invisible in the calm, the gray man goes.
> Do you not sense (*or* hear *or* feel) the
>   dead? But the earth is deaf.

This poem, the first of *Un río, un amor,* is presumably the earliest, and demonstrates its transitional nature by formal regularity, on the one hand and, on the other by the distinctly surrealist properties (the invisible gray man, aimless wandering, wings, emptiness, the cryptic phrases). I have adopted a stanza of three iambic tetrameter lines and a fourth of iambic pentameter.

Exile

The last two lines rendered literally are:

Night abandons him and dawn finds him,
Behind his tracks the shadow stubbornly.

The final, "floating" adverb seems meant to suggest, by its syntactical disconnectedness, the doggedness of the exile's personal history: it follows him like the light of daybreak, and, grammatically, is represented without a verb, but as an implied permanent state, almost actionless.

Sleep, Child

The title in Spanish specifies, "Sleep, Boy."

Literally,

> The fury of death, the tortured bodies,
> The revolution, (a) fan in one's hand,
> Impotence of the powerful (one), hunger of the
>   thirsty (one),
> Doubt with hands of doubt and feet of doubt;
>
> Sadness, shaking its necklaces
> In order to cheer up a bit so many old ones;
> All united (*or* all one) among tombs like
>   stars,
> Among lubricities (*or* sensualities,
>   luxuriousnesses) like moons;
> Death, the passion in the tresses,
> Sleep (*or* doze) as miniscule as a tree,
> Sleep as small or as large
> As a tree grown until reaching the ground.
>
> Today however he too is tired.

The English translation is more specific, and more interpretive therefore, than a "literal" version. The poem is an upside-down lullaby, lulling the child to sleep not with pleasantries but with a catalog of doom, both social and individual. Even the tree grows upside down.

Nocturne Among Grotesqueries

"Musarañas" are vermin, or little puppets or dolls of a grotesque sort; one also asks, in Spanish, "¿Estás mirando a musarañas?" to mean "Are you day-dreaming?"

Literally,

> Body of stone, sad body
> Between wools like walls of (the) universe,
> Identical to the races when they have a
>   birthday,
> To the most innocent edifices,
> To the most modest waterfalls,
> (Which are) white like the night, while the
>   mountain
> Tears up crazed forms
> Tears up pains (*or* griefs) like fingers,
> Joys like fingernails
> Not knowing where to go, where to return to,
> Searching for the pious winds
> That destroy the wrinkles of the world,
> That bless the desires cut (out) at the root
> Before giving their flower,
> Their flower large like a child.
>
> The lips want that flower
> Whose fist, kissed by the night,
> Opens the doors of oblivion (*or*
>   forgetfulness; the realm of the forgotten)
>   lip by lip.

A poem of solitude, perhaps of autoeroticism; as difficult a poem as Cernuda wrote. It may also suggest something of the procreative frustration of the homosexual.

I Will Tell How You Were Born

This poem which opens the collection *Forbidden Pleasures*, is an ideological autobiography; that is, it both

accounts for the development of the "forbidden plea-
sures" by telling of the circumstances of their birth, and
announces its categorical opposition to those circum-
stances. The link between sexual and political rebellion
is explicit here (lines 23-28, 42-51 of the translation), as
well as the link between pleasure and annihilation (line
46).

As a corrupt and decaying society is elliptically por-
trayed, so forbidden pleasures are presented not as an
escape from that society but as rebellion. Marcuse is
relevant, if I may be permitted to quote him at length:

> The [sexual] perversions thus express rebellion against the
> subjugation of sexuality under the order of procreation,
> and against the institutions which guarantee this order.
> Psychoanalytic theory sees in the practices that exclude or
> prevent procreation an opposition against continuing the
> chain of reproduction and thereby of paternal domina-
> tion — an attempt to prevent the "reappearance of the
> father." The perversions seem to reject the entire enslave-
> ment of the pleasure ego by the reality ego. Claiming
> instinctual freedom in a world of repression, they are often
> characterized by a strong rejection of that feeling of guilt
> which accompanies sexual repression. . . . Against a society
> which employs sexuality as means for a useful end, the
> perversions uphold sexuality as an end in itself. . . . They
> are a symbol . . . of the destructive identity between free-
> dom and happiness.
>
> [*Eros and Civilization* (New York, 1962), pp. 45-46]

Cernuda presents a destructiveness aimed at the estab-
lished repression of libido and erotic gratification, at
imposed limits on all activities, and at everything *felt* as
inhibiting. This poem is perhaps of all Cernuda's poetry
the most susceptible of explicit Freudian analysis; at the
same time, it is not entirely a characteristic poem.

The most difficult aspect of the poem is the tone,
which seems to be at times sarcastically directed out-
ward, at times grandiose, self-justifying, directed inward.
Thus, line 8 could be the sort of violent and even

narcissistic self-mutilation one sees in Lafcadio Wluiki in Gide's *Les Caves du Vatican* (and see Cernuda's essay "Carta a Lafcadio Wluiki" — written in 1931! — *Poesía y Literatura,* pp. 367-371), or a sardonic mimicking of what is implicit in repressive society.

Line 18 (English translation): the fallen regime is most likely the monarchy.

19: the oxymoron conveys the total disjunction between the forbidden pleasures and the world they inhabit.

29: the paper limits may be the limits of legal power of a king whose government was legally superseded by an elected Republic. Whether the implied identification of the rebellion of youth with the new, conquering Republic is justified, is not here at issue: for intellectuals, the mood during the Republic's first days was jubilant and unrestrained.

51: the line is problematic, since *vuestro* has before referred to the forbidden pleasures, but here seems to be aimed, suddenly, at an audience.

The Mind is Hung with Cobwebs

Line 1: *razón* is literally "reason," but by implication is the whole mind, in Spanish, whereas "reason" seems narrower in English.

10: Unlike English, Spanish need not specify gender in this construction. If the "forbidden pleasures" of this volume mean anything, they require that English give "his" for *su.*

He Did Not Speak Words

As else where, English must specify gender here, in the title and in the first lines, where the Spanish need not.

17: An allusion to Aristophanes' explanation of love in Plato's *Symposium.*

Bodies Like Flowers

The final stanza is remarkable for the predominance of the subjunctive mood, which cannot be translated fluently into English.

Passion for Passion

Again, the Spanish leaves the gender of "pleasure" unspecified, although pleasure is personified. English must give the gender. That *placer* is a masculine noun does not determine the case, but in Spanish does reinforce the reader's surmise that pleasure is a man, a male figure of chaos and destruction as well as of gratification: two sides of Eros.

II

The syntax of the English translation varies in several instances from Cernuda's Spanish syntax, which is extremely extended. Literally,

As one sail on the sea
Sums up that blue longing that rises
As far as the future stars,
Made (a) staircase of waves
Where divine feet descend to the abyss,
Also your very form,
Angel, demon, dream of a dreamed love,
Sums up in me a longing which in another time raised
As far as the clouds its melancholy waves.

Feeling still the pulses of that longing,
I, the most enamored,
On the shores of love,
Without (there being) a light that might see
    me
Definitively dead or alive,
(I) contemplate its waves and wish to sink in
    them,

Desiring hopelessly (*or* desperately)
To descend, like those angels on the stairs of
    sea-foam,
Down to the depths of love itself which no man has
    seen.

The Poet's Glory

Line 1: It seemed strongest and quite acceptable to translate *mi semejante* back into its unmistakable origin, "mon semblable," from Baudelaire's "Au Lecteur."

43: *aterciopeladamente* ("Oh so gently" in the translation, but literally "velvetly"), if not a neologism, is sufficiently unusual, not to say grotesque, to seem one. Here its effect is to reinforce the ridiculousness and posing of the philistines who torture their children, speaking in a baby-language, perhaps, and who pretend sensitivity to the natural world as if it, and not they, were a violation of the proper order of things. Above, lines 36-38 (translation), introduce this idea.

65: "the tortuous mountains near the capital" would be the Sierra Guadarrama north of Madrid, traditional retreat of city residents, the site of second, "weekend" houses for many.

To A Dead Poet

F. G. L. is Federico García Lorca, who was executed shortly after the outbreak of the war in 1936 by the Nationalist command in Granada, the city of his birth, to which he had returned from Madrid for sanctuary from the inevitable and imminent armed struggle. Such executions were so common as to become the "normal" practice of the repressive military government of the Nationalists, especially in Andalucía, which Franco's forces quickly controlled. Now it is clear that almost all intellectuals within reach of the military and police forces there were imprisoned or executed for their suspected anti-Franco activities. Lorca was shot along with a schoolteacher, and neither of them was really an active political man. (See Ian Gibson, *The Death of Lorca* [Chicago, 1973].) But Cernuda and other intellectuals outside Granada assumed that Lorca's execution was meant as reprisal against a poet specifically, and thus against art, against mind and spirit. They would have been shocked further had they known that in Granada the execution of Lorca was almost without distinction, and certainly part of a routine.

90: *Afán,* a frequent word in Cernuda's poems, seems here to refer back to the *afán* of lines 53 and 56. But whereas the "longing" in those earlier lines seems to be of the broadest sort — an alienation of all men from each other and from the world, which is yet *oculto,* "hidden," it is also a reference to homosexuality, as is apparent in stanza six. (*Oculto* is similarly used in the poem "Clandestine Love".) Thus in line 90, Lorca's own *gran afán enajenado* is both sexual and vocational — the toil of his poetic calling. This correspondence is also established by Cernuda in "I Will Tell How You Were Born," and implicitly informs much of his thinking about the alienation of the poet, and the poet's life among philistines. It is important not to call too much attention to homosexuality in Cernuda's life and work, nor, on the other hand, to slight it as one determining element in his living and writing.

Common Sense

The title comes from Spanish *cuerdo,* meaning sane, sensible, which in turn derives from Latin *Cordatus.* That the heart is the seat of the sort of common sense of which Cernuda writes is most significant here.

Impression of Exile

Here again the reader meets Lazarus, this time as a Spanish exile.

Stanza three presents some difficulty in the words *sombra* and *asomarse.* The latter means literally to rise into sight, and here it is the former, "shadow," which does so. Literally,

> I saw
> The shadow of his long profile a few times
> Rise into sight, abstracted(ly) at the
>   edge of the cup. . . .

Stanza four, literally:
> On someone's lips
> Over in the corners
> Where the old ones buzzed together,
> (As) dense as a falling tear,
> One word suddenly surged forth: Spain.

Line 40: The third edition of *La realidad y el deseo* (1958) gives:

> Como si fuera solo bajo un peso invisible

and I have adopted this reading in the English translation for the added weight of the word "alone."

Gulls in the Parks

Set presumably in London. Literally:

> Mistress of workshops, factories, bars,
> All dark stones beneath a dark sky,
> Silent to the night, devout on Sundays,
> It is the levitical city which denies its
>   sins.
>
> The muddy green of grass and trees
> Interrupts with (its) parks the uniform
>   buildings,
> And in the charmless nature, in the rain,
> (You) suddenly see, a panache of madness, the
>   gulls.
>
> Why, having wings, are they the guests of
>   smoke,

The dirty stream, the wooden bridges of these
    parks?
A wind of misfortune or an unconscious hand
Brought them inland from their native ports.

The nest of the seas remained far behind,
    shaken by storms
Of winter, in luminous calm in summers.
Now their lament goes, like the cry of souls
    in exile.
He who made them with wings, denies them
    space.

The translation of this poem in the Anthony Edkins and
Derek Harris edition, which is by Edward Wilson, gives
"pharasaical city" for line 4. Assuming that this is one
of the translations that Wilson and Cernuda worked on
together, I have taken that reading for my translation
also, for "levitical city" is puzzling. (*The Poetry of Luis
Cernuda* [New York, 1971], p. 87.)

A Spaniard Speaks of His Land

Line 2: The reminiscence is even stronger if one recalls
the second poem of *A River, A Love,* "Quisiera estar
solo en el sur" ("I Want to be Alone in the South"),
which begins:

Quizá mis lentos ojos no verán más el
    sur
De ligeros paisajes dormidos en el aire.

Perhaps my lethargic eyes will never see again
The south — the delicate landscapes asleep in
    the air.

And the third poem of that volume, "Sombras Blancas"
("White Shadows") begins thus:

Sombras frágiles, blancas, dormidas en la
    playa,
Dormidas en su amor . . .

Fragile shadows, white, asleep on the beach,
Asleep in their love . . .

[(*La realidad y el deseo,* pp. 41-42)]

Ruins

In stanza eleven, the address to the second person
changes direction. Formerly it was God whom the poet
addressed as *tú*; now it is himself, all men. In the English,
I have reworded the sentence so that it addresses man
indirectly, substituting the third person for the second.

Native Land

Set in Andalucía.

Line 22: *amor* could be "love" the emotional state or
"love" the beloved. To "conquer" the former would not
be the same as to conquer the latter — an ambiguity
apparently intended.

23: *lo,* "it," here means "dream" or "memory," while
line 24, "the more mine," refers to the native land.

Apologia pro vita sua

Cernuda does not mention having read Cardinal New-
man, but it seems to me that Cernuda's "Historial"
resembles to some extent Newman's *Apologia* in the
way it emphasizes its author's reactions to certain
books. Also, Cernuda may have been drawn across what
I would take to be a chasm of temperamental and
philosophical differences toward a writer whose concern
for self-examination and sincerity was very like his own.
A sense of vocation is common to both men, as is the
degree to which each regards his vocation as exclusive,
entirely overriding other claims or interests. Cernuda's
religious concern in this poem is hardly less than New-
man's, especially since, as Newman recounts a con-
version, so Cernuda suggests that his early attitudes
toward Christianity are now somewhat altered; charac-
teristically, however, his desire for absolution takes the

form of musing on the sensual significance of extreme unction (see stanza eight).

The poem is not consistently repentant. Stanza seven is still rebellious and forceful, and the reflection on God's dependence on man is like similar thoughts in "The Visitation of God" or in "Ruins." The poem's conclusion is questioning, and at best merely hopeful.

Line 13: *contagiada* presents the same image found in the poem "Wind and Soul."

Stanza five alludes both to the cave in Plato's *Republic* and to the gates of horn and ivory in Book XIX of the Odyssey, from which true and false dreams issue, respectively.

The Cemetery

Line 1: *esparcir* means "to sprinkle," as when holy water is sprinkled from an aspergillum, and thus seems appropriate here, except for the ungainly difficulty it creates as a mixed metaphor with the greyhounds. Hence "scatters" in English.

Wind and Soul

Stanza one, literally:

> With such vehemence the wind
> Comes from the sea that its elemental
> Sounds infect
> The silence of the night.

Unfinished Statue

A prose poem from the first (London) edition of *Ocnos,* suppressed because of religious censorship in subsequent editions, gives another version of the threshold on which David-Apollo stands in this poem: "But childhood ended, and I fell into the world. People around me died, and houses went to ruin." (The prose poem, "Escrito en el agua," is reprinted in Cernuda, *Crítica,* pp. 195-197.)

And in "El tiempo," also from *Ocnos,* Cernuda writes: "A moment comes in life when time overtakes us. (I am not sure I express this properly.) I mean that after a certain age we see ourselves subject to time, and obliged to deal with it, as if some furious vision with flashing sword were to drive us from that first paradise where every man has once lived, free from the sting of death" (*Ocnos,* 3d ed. [Xalapa, México: Universidad Veracruzana, 1963], p. 29).